LIFE IS TOO SHORT TO SKIP PLANNING

1st edition

Copyright 2019 Riko H. A. Jr.

Published by Riko H. A. Jr.

LIFE IS TOO SHORT TO SKIP PLANNING

1st edition

Riko H. A. Jr.

Summary

To all who, without knowing it, have taught me so much...

"Would you tell me, please, which way I ought to go from here?" Alice asked the Cheshire Cat.

"That depends a good deal on where you want to get to" answered the Cat.

"I don't much care where" said Alice

"Then, it doesn't really matter which way you go, does it?"

CHAPTER ONE

Choosing a destination

Biarritz region, Basque Country, France

June 14th, 2017

Na Pali – the name of a Hawaiian island was also the name of the building that served as the Headquarters of Quiksilver in the city of Saint-Jean-de-Luz in the Southwest of France.

Surfboards and snowboards in the walls and ceilings decorated the building all made of wood, almost hidden by a forest of pines. The architect who designed it received an award of the best building in Europe for it. It had been designed to bring an environment of well-being that surfers could appreciate.

I was right in the middle of my 6-months trainee contract, a requirement for the conclusion of my MBA.

Man, I was living the dream!

Working at Quiksilver and the quality of life in the French Basque Country were unimaginable! Work was just a 5 minutes car ride away. I worked from 9:30 to 6 pm, in a 35-hour workweek with an hour and a half long lunch break when everyone took time to play some kind of sport. Some people would go for a run, others swam, skated, played soccer or if waves were good, most of us would pick our surfboards and just cross the street to go surf in Lafitenia, a beach endowed with the best waves of the region.

This day there was a party going on in the evening to present the new collection. The models paraded inside Agora, the large central hall that linked the various buildings of the headquarters.

A large screen inside Agora was showing the surf championship live from Fiji where Matt Wilkinson and Connor O'Leary were face to face in one of the best waves in the planet, and I was outside in that warm evening of June in Southwest of France, listening to Tom Curren playing a nice and easy surf music on his guitar.

For those who do not remember, Curren is a three-time world champion, a kind of a "Kelly Slater" of the late 80s.

All the details of that evening remain fresh in my mind, from the smell of the flowers at the end of spring, the sound of the music that Curren was playing to the taste of the Caipirinha I was drinking.

And I had a feeling of completion: I made it, I had it all!

But then, while I was twisting the glass of my caipirinha, a thought hit my mind for the first time: what's next?

Life wasn't over, and I had inside me a need to accomplish something bigger. You know I found the life I always dreamt of and I was puzzle because honestly, what could be wrong with living close to nice beaches, have time to surf every day, and be sure that nothing wrong would never happen to your kids? Nothing was wrong with that. But, for the weeks that followed, that thought got deeper and deeper.

I, my wife, Alice, and our older daughter, Anna, had moved to France about a year before that. When we arrived in France for my MBA, Alice found out she was pregnant. We were living in the beautiful, casual but chic city of Bordeaux, hometown of the best wines in the world.

Even though I was working very hard in my studies, we had time to spend together, something we never had before moving to France. This period was a game changer in my life. Our original plans were to return back home once I'd finish my MBA, but we didn't want to. We loved our life in France so much that we decided to stay and give it a try.

It was a moment of deep reflection for me.

It was a big move. I needed to decide what I wanted for my life, so that we were sure that the decision we would take would be in the right direction. This was the first time that I'd taken a moment to plan my entire life going forward. Time flies, and you have no choice, it will pass it anyway whether you plan it or not.

I had learned a lot about planning through my career in Finance and I realized how important it was.

But honestly in my younger years, I must confess, I was not known as the "planning guy". When I was young, I simply hated planning anything. I would say a simple yes to whatever someone would invite me to do and then try to make it, but with no engagement at all. I was late for basically all of them and did not confirm my attendance until the very last minute. If you asked any of my friends, they'll surely confirm what a nightmare it was to get me to attend anything.

I simply hated any type of commitment!

I had a "planning phobia." I would rather not know, not schedule, and just let things happen by themselves...

I felt that once I committed to something, even if it was a bar with friends, it would no longer be that fun. It would be a compromise! What if I was tired on Friday night? What if it is rainy and I feel like staying home watching movies on TV? What if someone else shows up with a better invitation?

Once, when I was in a graduate talent program in my former company, I completed the Myers–Briggs Type Indicator - known as MBTI - personality test. One of my traces was a strong "P" (that stands for Perceiving). "P" people are casual, open-ended, prompted, spontaneous and emergent.

The opposite of "P" is "J", of Judging. People that are diagnosed as systematic, planful, early starting, scheduled, methodical.

I was so "P" that my friends would just remind me of that fact every time I was acting in a too "P" way.

That was me.

Today, I am author of Financial Planning books, I work with Corporate Financial Planning and in my articles, I talk about the importance of planning.

I changed, evolved and in the end, I have transformed the mess that my life had always been by using something that today I do not know if I could ever live without: planning.

Once I found it, I saw how rewarding it was. It can be part of people's personality, I agree. But, if not, it is still possible to learn and change.

There is no evolution without changes. But it is a continuous effort. First you must decide to change. It all starts in our brains: who and where do you want to be in the future?

The next step is planning and then, the most important: attitude.

As Rachel Dawes would say, it's not who we are underneath that defines us, but what we do! We are the reflex of our attitudes and that is how my planning history begins, with profound changes over time. One step at a time, but always straight on. A bit like Bruce Wayne traumatized by falling into a pit with bats, and that ended with him making the bat the symbol of his power.

When we identify a weakness in ourselves and we decide to strive to change it, along the way it may become our strength.

Now, I want to help others find what I found.

The Australian futurist Peter Ellyard says we cannot create a future we did not initially imagined. That is precisely what planning is: it is creating the future. Planning is not a guessing game, it's about decisions and compromise.

Back to my days in Biarritz, one of my plans was to write a book about Financial Planning that could serve as a tool to anyone willing to organize his or her financial life.

Most of the financial books at that time were more like motivational books. Well, nothing wrong with that, they are all great books, but there was no guidebook that shows you all the steps of how to organize your financial life.

I was trying to find my way, so I began to write my future in the form of a script of my life. It was the first time I've done it.

In parallel, I was receiving several requests from friends to write a book about Investments. It was definitely not a bad idea.

As soon as I decided to go for it, the scope grew bigger as I started to deep dive into the main reasons why people have money issues. A lot of whys came into my head as I tried to find out the root causes of why people struggle with their finances.

To start with, in order to invest, first you must have savings to do so. Not everyone does. Why? Because they lack the simple budgeting skills.

And why is that? One reason is because they did not learn that in school. Why? Because society decides the curriculum and apparently it is not a priority to teach kids how to deal with money.

We can still learn things by ourselves, especially nowadays that books, e-books, videos etc. are more available than ever. But as incredible as it might sound, most people think their own lives don't depend on themselves. If they are unhappy at work, it is their boss' fault. If they have no quality of life, it is the politicians' fault, the bankers'... you name it. Everything that happens in their lives is the fault of somebody else other than their own. In their minds, they are not guilty of anything, they are simply victims of the outside world. Because for them, life "just happens."

Why would they bother planning if in the end, they feel their lives depend more on other people than themselves? Besides, some people don't have a good relationship with money because they see it as a source of unfairness, injustice and greed. Others, because they see a trade-off between living life and living an organized financial life.

There are many reasons why people have a bad relationship with money. I am going to explore them all here, in the following order:

- excuses for not thinking about your financial life
- show your place in the economic world
- discuss what is your role in your own life
- make you think about behavioral economic decision making
- present you how to plan and control your financial life
- and give you a long-term easy-to-apply investment strategy

I will also share with you in the end of this book my own Planning & Control Excel template so that you can either use it or have some ideas to help adjust yours.

This is not a self-help book kind of style though, I won't promise you'll automatically turn into a millionaire just by placing your hand on your heart and saying it out loud. I also don't promise you'll never order chicken again. By the way, I love chicken!

What I'll show you here is how you should think about your financial life, I'll bring real cases and tips from getting rid of debt to controlling your monthly budget and investing. I will talk a lot about behavior and mindset because without these you'll certainly get stuck.

Knowledge is the only possible way to build a healthy financial life. No one knows so much to the point that there is nothing else to learn and no one knows so little that there is nothing to teach. Everyone has something to contribute in this world.

My "something" is here. I'm here to share with you everything I've learned.

Let's get started!

CHAPTER TWO

Life is too short to skip planning

"Remembering that I'll be dead soon is the most important tool I've ever encountered to help me make the big choices in life.

Almost everything - all external expectations, all pride, all fear of embarrassment or failure - these things just fall away in the face of death, leaving only what is truly important.

Remembering that you are going to die is the best way I know to avoid the trap of thinking you have something to lose.

You are already naked.

There is no reason not to follow your heart.

No one wants to die. Even people who want to go to heaven don't want to die to get there. And yet, death is the destination we all share. No one has ever escaped it, and that is how it should be, because death is very likely the single best invention of life. It's life's change agent. It clears out the old to make way for the new." (Steve Jobs speech in Stanford, 2005)

I believe that we all agree with Steve Jobs' words. It makes sense, it's logical. But, when it comes to action, most people revert the logic.

Curiously, not knowing when we'll die has turned into one of the most popular excuses for not planning, and ultimately, not accomplishing anything great in life. Instead of moving them forward, most people use it to hold them back.

For some people, planning means counting on being alive in the future to benefit from the sacrifices made today and since no one can guarantee that this will be the case, it is best not to plan, not to invest. In reality – they say - you can die tomorrow and can't take anything from this world with you.

If we imagine this excuse applied for all aspects in life other than financial planning, we end up not creating anything.

Why would one spend years studying at a University questioning if he will be alive to benefit from this investment?

Why engage in long-term mortgages without knowing if the property will ever really be yours?

And on top of that, "tomorrow" is so close that you can even wonder why people work the entire month without being sure they will be alive to receive their salaries at the end of the month.

It surprises me how this excuse is used almost exclusively to avoid financial organization.

I've been hearing it for a long time and I've always answered with another question: "Okay, but what if you are unlucky enough and survive the next day?"

Surviving should not be considered bad luck, but some people seem to strive for this to be the case. The future they create has only two options: die or live life without creating anything valuable!

What is wrong with this people?

I'll tell you what is wrong, this excuse is only a way of trying to justify the actions generated by the consumerism and since they don't want to admit that what they lack is real interest in controlling their lives, they seek a "rational" justification for their behavior.

But there has always been those who think differently.

One of the periods of greatest evolutions in human history was the Agricultural Revolution about 10,000 years ago, called the Neolithic period.

Thinking about the human existence, that was yesterday.

For thousands of years human groups have been moving from one place to another, looking for food necessary for their survival.

They were nomadic groups that depended exclusively on hunting and collecting fruits and vegetables in nature.

The beginning of agriculture was a real revolution in man's way of life. When we decided to plant our own food, we no longer needed to move constantly in search of survival. The first fixed societies were organized and Men could protect themselves.

Once the activity started, it became possible to learn how to select the best plants for sowing and to promote grafting, in order to produce more nutritious foods than the ones found in the wild.

Men grew stronger and chances of survival increased.

Everything that has happened in terms of technological, economic and social evolution would not have been possible if the agricultural revolution had not occurred there at that moment.

It was at this age that we began to create the basis for the concept of cities, professions and ultimately the world as we know today.

Jared Diamond in Guns, Germs and Steel: The Fates of human societies says: "Twelve thousand years ago, everybody was a hunter-gatherer; now almost all of us are farmers or else fed by farmers."

At that time, everyone's goal was to fight for survival. Agriculture was a disruption by generating a surplus of food. Now, with at least a certain amount of food for survival kind of guaranteed, we could start thinking and doing other activities.

This freedom from having to forage or farm allowed people to become scholars, craftsmen and traders. While some would work to put food on our tables, others would work building these tables.

But even during the agricultural revolution, many unbelievers in this new technology and way of seeing life remained nomads for the rest of their lives, organizing themselves into tribes, apart from this new world that emerged.

The point is, that planting your own food is risky and is a long-term objective. You should be aware that the results of the harvest will not be available for consumption in the next day - and sometimes never.

There is not always the correct amount of rain when you need it the most. The characteristics of the soil may not be appropriate to grow the seeds that you planted.

It is necessary to wait, to be patient and have faith to continue cultivating, day after day, irrigating and treating the land even if the benefit of this work is not immediate. There are crops that take many months from planting to harvesting. In addition, it is an intense trial and error game with no guarantee that it will work.

The irony is that there are many uncertainties we have to face to achieve safety.

Now, imagine if everyone at that time wondered if they would be alive until the harvest and the fact that they were all going to die one day prevented them from growing the first crops?

10,000 years ago, investors were born, revolutionaries with a long-term vision and a valuable lesson for any of us today.

This lesson is still valid. It is necessary to plant, to take care, to persist every day, to harvest.

Evolution is a consequence.

For some this may require a greater dose of optimism than it is natural and even if a minimum of optimism is a prerequisite for building anything in life, it is true that it is not a common characteristic of all of us.

But it doesn't even have to be.

If we look at this in a more rational way, we will conclude that "dying tomorrow" is not even highly probable.

As I said at the beginning of the chapter, it is a fact that we will all die someday, but I'll tell you this: it will not be tomorrow.

With all the certainty of the world? Of course not, because dying is always a possibility both today and tomorrow or the day after tomorrow.

But while totally possible, it is at least unlikely that it will be tomorrow.

Come on...

Life expectancy in the world today is 72 years according to the United Nations data.

And it varies a lot from country to country. Below a list of life expectancy around the world:

Country	Life expectancy
Japan	84
Italy	83
Australia	83
Canada	82
France	82
United Kingdom	81
Germany	81
United States	79
Mexico	77
China	76
Brazil	76
Russia	70
India	68

Just to give you an idea, in 1950, life expectancy in the world was about 50 years.

Can you imagine that?

It is an enormous increase.

Even the concept of "old men and women" itself has changed. Compared to my grandparents' generation, my parents are young people in their 60's and 70's.

There are several reasons that explain our longevity increase from medicinal advances to increased concern about health and well-being.

In the US, for example, where life expectancy is 79 years you must be thinking: someone of this age is coming close to his/her time, right?

Not really.

Americans who have reached the age of 79, have an expectation of living for an additional 10 years on average. If you have reached 79, chances are great to live until 89.

This is called the expectation of survival.

In fact, what we usually call life expectancy is called life expectancy at birth.

An American baby who has just been born into the world is expected to live on average for 79 years.

But, unfortunately, infant mortality (babies who do not complete the first year) is large, the average is decreased.

The older you get your chances of aging more and more only increase.

According to the most recent data, those who reach the age of 20 live on average up to 80 in the US. At 40, life expectancy increases to 81 years. At 50, it goes up to 82. At 60, it jumps to 83. At 70, it goes to 85. And at 80, the expectation is to live until you are 89.

All this, on average. There are those who die before their time, victims of accidents, urban violence and fatal diseases, but today the vast majority of us reach old age. It is a fact: we are all living longer.

Of course, we are all going to die one day, and we do not know when. It may be even tomorrow, but statistics show something different. And unless you are in a delicate health situation, the chances of surviving the next day will always be greater than the chances of dying, even if death is certain for all of us.

There's a cute quote that says "if you live every day as if it were the last, one day you'll be right."

I say, sure, one day you will be right, but you will live all the other days of your life in the wrong way.

But don't get me wrong here, remembering that we are going to die one day can be very useful for most of our decisions in life. It can be a great force that will pull us forward, but it can also be a bad excuse for holding us back and not allowing us to build anything valuable in our lives.

Life is long enough to accomplish great things if we execute our plans. But there must be plans to be executed. Otherwise, time just slips away, and you'll find yourself locked in a never-ending routine until one day you wake up and realize your life just went by. Gone.

So, take note of this: You most likely won't die tomorrow, but you'll surely die one day. Realize that and use it in your favor. There is still time for accomplishment, but you have to start moving the needle forward today.

A 90-Year Human Life in Months

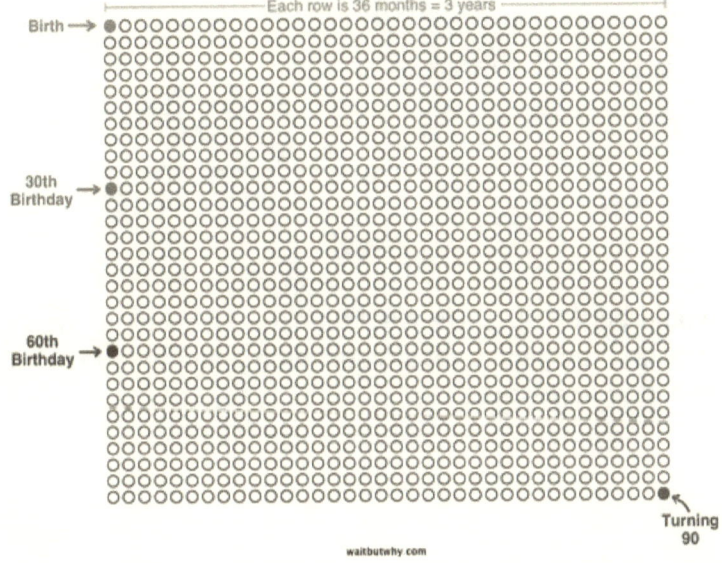

waitbutwhy.com

The graph above is what Tim Urban calls a Life Calendar. Each box represents a month of a 90-years life.

As you can see, there aren't that many boxes in that graph, especially considering that we've already used a bunch of them. Take a long, hard look at that calendar. We need to think about what things we're skipping here, because I am pretty sure each one of us is missing something that wanted to have done in life.

That's a job for all of us. And because there's not that many boxes left there, start planning and accomplishing is a job you probably better start today.

This was all presented by Tim in one of my favorite Tedx Talks ever. In the same show, he spoke about the time he used to be a government major, having to constantly write a lot of papers. He would plan and spread the work out a little like the graph below.

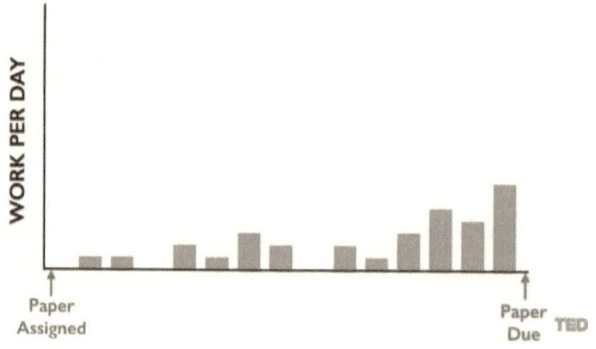

That would be the plan. He would have it all ready to go, but then, actually, the paper would come along, and then in reality he would kind of do this:

And that would happen every single paper.

Then it came his 90-page senior thesis, a paper one is supposed to spend a year on. He knew for a paper like that, his normal workflow was not an option. It was way too big a project. So, he planned things like this:

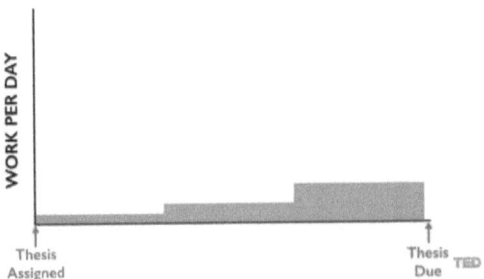

This is how the year would go. So, he would start off light and bump it up in the middle months, and then at the end, he would kick it into high gear, just like a little staircase. But then, the first few months came and went, and he couldn't quite do stuff. And then one day he woke up with three days until the deadline, still not having written a word.

So, he did the only thing he could have done: he wrote the 90 pages over 72 hours, sprinted across campus, dove in slow motion, and got it in just at the deadline.

The question is how can a guy spend a full year not being able to write one single sentence finish a 90-pages thesis in 3 days?

Tim has become a writer-blogger and decided to write about procrastination. His goal is to explain to the non-procrastinators of the world what goes on in the heads of procrastinators, and why they are the way they are. His hypothesis is that the brains of procrastinators are actually different than the brains of other people. And to test this, he found an MRI lab that actually let he scan both the brain of two people: one procrastinator and one who was not.

He was correct and his research pointed out that actually the two brains are quite different. So, here's the brain of a non-procrastinator:

Now, here's the brain of a procrastinator.

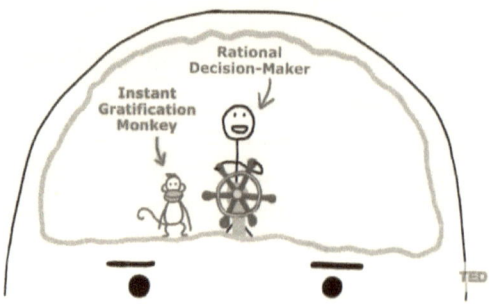

There is a difference.

Both brains have a rational decision-maker in them, but the procrastinator's brain also has an instant gratification monkey.

Now, what does this mean for the procrastinator? Well, it means everything is fine until the instant gratification monkey takes control.

So, the rational decision-maker will make the rational decision to do something productive, but the monkey doesn't like that plan, so he takes the wheel, and he says, actually, let's read the entire Wikipedia page of the Nancy Kerrigan/Tonya Harding scandal, because I just remembered that that happened.

Then he's going to go over to the fridge to see if there's anything new in there since 10 minutes ago. After that, he is going to go on a YouTube spiral that starts with videos of Richard Feynman talking about magnets and ends much, much later with him watching interviews with Justin Bieber's mom.

"All of that's going to take a while, so we're not going to really have room on the schedule for any work today. Sorry!" the monkey says.

Now, what is going on there? The Instant Gratification Monkey does not seem like a guy you want behind the wheel. He lives entirely in the present moment. He has no memory of the past, no knowledge of the future, and he only cares about two things: easy and fun.

Now, in the animal world, that works fine. If you're a dog and you spend your whole life doing nothing other than easy and fun things, you're a huge success! And to the Monkey, humans are just another animal species. You have to keep well-slept, well-fed and propagating into the next generation, which in tribal times might have worked OK.

But, if you haven't noticed, now we're not in tribal times. We're in an advanced civilization, and the Monkey does not know what that is. Which is why we have another guy in our brain, the Rational Decision-Maker, who gives us the ability to do things no other animal can do. We can visualize the future. We can see the big picture. We can make long-term plans. And he wants to take all of that into account. And he wants to just have us do whatever makes sense to be done right now.

Sometimes it makes sense to be doing things that are easy and fun, like when you're having dinner or going to bed or enjoying well-earned leisure time. That's why there's an overlap. Sometimes the monkey and the rational decision-maker agree. But other times, it makes much more sense to be doing things that are harder and less pleasant, for the sake of the big picture. And that's when there is a conflict.

For the procrastinator, that conflict tends to end a certain way every time, leaving him spending a lot of time in the easy and fun zone that is entirely out of the Makes Sense circle. This place is known as the Dark Playground.

The Dark Playground is a place that all procrastinators know very well. It's where leisure activities happen at times when leisure activities are not supposed to be happening.

The fun you have in the Dark Playground isn't actually fun because it's completely unearned, and the air is filled with guilt, dread, anxiety, self-hatred — all of those good procrastinator feelings.

And the question is, in this situation, with the Monkey behind the wheel, how does the procrastinator ever get himself over to the correct zone, a less pleasant place, but where really important things happen?

Well, turns out the procrastinator has a guardian angel, someone who's always looking down on him and watching over him in his darkest moments. That someone is called the Panic Monster.

The Panic Monster

waitbutwhy.com

The Panic Monster is dormant most of the time, but he suddenly wakes up anytime a deadline gets too close or there's danger of public embarrassment, a career disaster or some other scary consequences. And importantly, he's the only thing that the Monkey is terrified of.

The Panic Monster explains all kinds of pretty insane procrastinator behavior, like how someone could spend two weeks unable to start the opening sentence of a paper, and then miraculously find the unbelievable work ethic to stay up all night and write eighty pages.

And this entire situation, with the three characters (the Rational Decision Maker, the Instant Gratification Money and the Panic Monster) is the procrastinator's system. It's not pretty, but in the end, it works.

So far, everything looks funny and – even if it's not the most productive system in the world – it also seems to just work fine.

Well, not quite.

Everything we have just talked about, all these examples had deadlines and when there's deadlines the effects of procrastination are contained to the short term because the Panic Monster gets involved.

But there's a second kind of procrastination that happens in situations when there is no deadline. And usually, this is the case for the most important things of life. So, if you want to get fit, spend more time with your family, get your financial life in shape, travel the world or become an entrepreneur, things get complicated. There are no deadlines on those things because nothing's happening at first, not until you've gone out and done the hard work to get momentum, to get things going.

Now if the procrastinator's only mechanism of doing these hard things is the Panic Monster, that's a problem because in all of these non-deadline situations, the Panic Monster doesn't show up.

He has nothing to wake up for, so the effects of procrastination, they're not contained; they just extend outward forever. And it's this long-term kind of procrastination that's much less visible and much less talked about than the funnier, short-term deadline-based kind. It's usually suffered quietly and privately. And it can be the source of a huge amount of long-term unhappiness, and regrets.

Years go by and when they realize how they have been spending their lives, they become frustrated. And it is not that they couldn't achieve their dreams; it's that they weren't even able to start chasing them.

So, knowing that we all are going to die can be either a powerful tool to help you start moving the needle forward or it can be an excuse for not even trying. It is up to you.

Regarding those who constantly use the expression "what if I die tomorrow?" for justifying their short-term oriented actions, rather than the lack of optimism or statistical inaccuracy, what surprises me the most is the selfish view of those who believe that consuming immediately the little they have built up is a mechanism of defense against the risk of leaving life without taking anything with them.

It is the fear of leaving to others what was built by them and the answer - stupid as I see it - is not to build anything.

Because great achievements need great efforts. It takes time.

My vision of the world has never been this one.

Between die trying to build something of value and live a lifetime without even trying, I definitely choose the former.

CHAPTER THREE

Understand your place in the economic world

A long time ago a king asked his cartographer to make a map of his kingdom. The map should be perfect and respect every detail of every single corner.

A few months later the cartographer then presented to the king a large map, but that by restriction of scale, was still very simplified for the king's taste.

The king then asked him to come back with map a lot more detailed.

Each time the cartographer returned; the king sent him back asking to include some new item as accurately as possible.

In the end, after years of hard work, the map was so perfect and reproduced so identically the reality that its size was so large that it covered the entire Kingdom.

It was when the king realized: that map had no use any longer.

Most people are not organized with money due to some unconscious money issues that they have not even realized yet.

It is obvious that if you don't think of money as a good thing, unconsciously, your mind will betray you in your pursuit of a better financial life.

The reason behind it is that most people don't understand how wealth is created. They see the economic world as a limited source of wealth in such a way that if someone is rich, that could only mean that his wealth was taken from others, and therefore a lot of other people will become poorer.

They don't see wealth for what it is: something that can be created from nothing. If someone becomes rich, usually, it is because this person has created wealth out of nowhere. Or almost nowhere.

Imagine you lived in an isolated island and suddenly had the idea of putting together some twigs and other pieces of trees to build yourself a handmade house. This is the miracle of the wealth creation! Where there wasn't pretty much anything of value, you, with creativity, initiative and hard work created something useful. That is wealth.

If you think now that there were more people living on this island, their lives wouldn't become harder just because now you became richer using your own means to create wealth. Come on, no one became poorer just because you used twigs to build yourself a place to sleep. No one gets poorer if you go chasing animals to eat or if you go fishing.

Not in an absolute way.

In a relative way, yes, of course. Now comparing one to another, it turns out that the ones with initiative become richer than the others.

But I am reluctant to accept wealth as a relative point of view as mine.

I find it jealous, miserable and selfish to think you become poorer just because someone else became richer. So, instead of being happy for somebody else's joy, you regret it not being you to have the same thing.

And plus, the courage to put up a new house can positively affect the rest of the people on that island, if they take it in a positive way, of course. It should inspire them all to do the same and build their own houses.

It's up to you to decide how to react to somebody else's success: you either take it as a personal offense or as an inspiration.

What would you rather do? Which way do you think generates better results?

The economy is not a closed box with limited source of wealth. Instead, the possibility of wealth creation is infinite. All it takes is imagination and courage to turn ideas into action.

One that creates something useful for someone is creating value, therefore, wealth. The sum of all the wealth created by each and every one of us is the total wealth of the world. All we can do is either cooperate to create wealth or just consume wealth created by others.

When thinking about economics you will get used to scenarios like "imagine that there is no government", "assuming there is no rest of the world", "let's say there was no financial market" and things like that.

The truth is that the world is so full of intricacies, small details and distractions that we often have to "turn them off" so that we can have a clearer understanding of its essence.

So, to try to simplify the society we live in, I suggest once again you imagine a group of people - let's say weary of global capitalism and wanting a simpler life - to flee to a desert island to set up an alternative society.

In the beginning, everyone would do a bit of everything for their own livelihood, until the challenges of survival arise and they realize that some people had more taste and aptitude for some tasks than others.

John could get 10 fishes at the same amount of time that Peter could only catch 5.

But when it comes to building huts, Peter's was much tougher and made a better one in less time.

With the difficulties, the days of hunger and homelessness, they realized that it would be wiser if each one focused on what they could do better.

By dividing the activities, professions were formed in the island.

As time went on, by doing the same job every day, these workers have specialized and become better at what they did.

With the experience gained, John's productivity in fishing increased. He began to understand how tides influence in fishing, he learned how to distinguish different types of fish and developed more effective networks.

Repetition leads to improvement and practice to perfection.

Now, thanks to the division of labor, as he was fully focused on it, John was able to catch enough fish to feed the entire island.

He became an expert on that.

Each one specialized in a specific activity and the total production of the island multiplied exponentially.

As a consequence, the exchanges arose. Each person exchanged what they had produced for something produced by someone else.

Since a direct barter is limited to two parties, they chose a common currency that would facilitate all these exchanges.

Gradually - by facing the natural difficulties of life - the alternative society evolved and became something very similar to everything it had left behind.

But now it was ok, as they all had experienced the challenges of survival, its members understood why things were the way they were. The reason why they left their society was more a lack of understanding how it works than because of its flaws.

This example briefly reflects a little of what Adam Smith wanted to get across in those pages of The Wealth of Nations of 1776, a landmark in the history of economics.

You have to understand what your role in this world is.

Start by your place in this example. If the world were to be summed up in this alternative society, what would be your role in it?

What are you currently producing in your life to trade for all these things that you consume every day? The food you eat, the house you live in, the car, utilities you consume, everything, they all have been produced for somebody else and you're able to consume it all in exchange for what you produce.

If these things were not produced directly by you, through your own effort, at least you must have produced something for the society that has an equivalent value. Otherwise you are living at the expense of someone else's effort.

The truth is that there is no magic in economy. If someone is receiving something without giving anything in return, it means that someone, somewhere, is producing without receiving.

It doesn't sound very fair, does it?

Many people wake up early every morning and go to work without being able to make the slightest connection between the reason why they are doing it and the standard of living they have.

This is naturally demotivating.

One of the main reasons why most people have problems in their financial lives is because they simply can't connect the dots.

In my simplified example, all these fishermen can think of is on apples, bananas and coconuts. They focus on what they want instead of on what they must produce in order to be able to receive back what they want.

They don't focus on what other people might need. And you know what? It's very simple! All other people need is more fresh fish.

If only everyone in life could just understand how more productive, they would be if they just focused on their "fishes".

So, focus on what you can produce and on the different ways you can become more productive in your job, in your company, etc.

Focus on your fish, and bananas, apples and coconuts will come easily as the reward.

It is no use thinking about the reward first.

People need what you have to give to them. There are a lot of people just waiting for your fish. Help them get what they want, and as a result, you'll get what you want.

This leads me to the major problem I identify in people these days and it can be summed up in a single word: entitlement. This is one of the biggest fears I have with my kids.

I come from a culture where I had a lot of examples of friends and even people in my family that were raised and constructed their lives around the belief that they were entitled to have a certain standard of living just because they were born in the family they were. So, because of that feeling of being naturally special they felt they were entitled to have a car when they turned 18, they had to live in a nice neighborhood for their entire lives, eat in nice places, go to restaurants, wear nice clothes, travel abroad etc. And plus, they would spend a huge amount of energy and time just trying to figure out what they loved to do and explaining everybody around how their work sucks, how poorly they are paid, and so on. Why? They feel they were born special as if there were something in their blood that would make them different from the others.

So, we grew up together, and you know, at some point we were all in the same level. I could see they looked at life in a different manner than I and my other friends did, but so far, we couldn't identify any different results coming from that.

But, as time passed by, it started to get harder for them to catch up with people they were raised with simply because as they felt so naturally entitled of having everything automatically perfect in their lives that no major nor college were good enough, then, no job was good enough, no boss was good enough, no paycheck – even in the beginning of their careers - was able to give them the kind of life they felt they deserved.

The missing point for them was that they were not giving anything to get the results they wanted back. And they had plenty of excuses for that. These people expect the entire world to understand the reasons why they are not delivering good results, but they are very loud when it's time to point out other people's imperfections. Job sucks, their boss sucks, banks suck, politicians suck.

I once heard one of my colleagues saying that he was currently paying to work because he was spending a lot more than his paycheck. Well, at that time he had just left college, so he was very junior, having the opportunity to work in an interesting department of a large company - and experience is certainly one of the greatest investments one can make early in the career - and more than that, at his age, he was apparently living by himself in a nice apartment in a nice neighborhood, owning a good new car and spending a lot of money on his credit card and travelling to Europe every year. He was not paying to work, he was just spending more than he was making. His parents were covering the rest.

The thing is that these people don't understand that what they make is linked to how much they deliver to society. We all have a role in society and the more impact you make in people's lives, the more you have it back in return.

You have to give value to this world before you receive anything back. This is a major concept. And I know, it is hard for some people to understand that, but unless you really start bringing value to society, maybe, you won't be able to live in the same neighborhood you were raised. You won't drive the same car as your other friends and won't travel for vacations every year.

One of Warren Buffet's son worked driving trucks in a farm, and there are a lot of different stories of how sons and daughters of successful people that worked hard using the skills they had. It's a different sense of meaning for wealth. Money is not everything in our lives, and there is nothing wrong about living with limited financial resources. The problem with most of these people that feel entitled is that they say they agree that "money is not everything", but they don't really feel it that way. They agree when they have to work and produce, but when the time comes to spend, magically money turns out to be very – very – important. Or what is worse, they could even insist on saying "money isn't important," what is important is to live in a nice house, eating in nice restaurants, travel, drive a nice car and enjoy all these nice things that only money can bring you. How hypocritical is that?

What I want my kids to learn is: what you are going to have back in your life is proportional to the value you are going to bring to other people's lives no matter if you are going to be an entrepreneur searching to bring new solutions for society's problems (that's what they do, right?) or an employee playing a role in somebody else's Engine. The main goal of all companies is to bring solutions to their consumers, whether their owners know it or not. And every task an employee performs should be important adding up to form the big picture that is helping the Company bring that solution.

Anna and Victoria, when reading this, please keep these words from your father in mind: you two are entitled to my love and my respect. The quality of life you'll have in the future will be related to the quality of life you'll help deliver to other people in the world.

CHAPTER FOUR

What is money?

We always want more, and we do not always realize that before enjoying more, we have to produce more.

Production is a natural challenge for humanity.

It is part of the struggle to survive.

It has always been like this. But today, it is sometimes difficult to realize it. We often get the impression of earning less than we deserve.

But what we earn has nothing to do with what we "deserve". The economy does not work like Santa Claus' list, handing out gifts to those who have behaved well throughout the year.

Being a good boy or having a degree from a reputed University doesn't automatically create wealth.

What we earn is related to the value of what we produce. If what you do is rare, useful and well known, there will be value.

So, the more you invest in yourself, the greater are your chances of producing something more valuable. It is not automatic, I repeat, a mere baker's degree will not be able to bake good bread by itself.

It is a match between preparation and attitude resulting in production.

Okay, very cool and enlightening, but then what's the role of money in all this engine?

Interesting question…

It is a common belief - crazy, by the way - that a piece of paper is capable of generating wealth, improving people's quality of life, giving them everything they want. Just like magic.

Crazy, I know, right?

Sorry to tell you: this is fake news.

That paper we keep in our wallets and we get used to calling money, in fact, is technically called "paper money" or banknotes.

It is not money. It's worth the money.

The amount of money in the economy is much higher than the amount of paper money in circulation.

Especially nowadays in which much of the operations take place through virtual transactions, internet banking, mobile apps and credit or debit cards.

These devices reduce the need for printed money.

In fact, many countries have lately even restricted the use of printed currency in their economies.

Paper money is nothing more than a check that comes pre-filled. It's a recognition that you have money. And money, in turn, is a credit you have with society.

In the past, most of the banknotes made clear that they could be exchanged for money.

A 1,000 Rupee banknote for example has the following sentence in it: "I promise to pay the bearer the sum of one thousand Rupees"

If paper money were money and money were wealth, it would be easy to end poverty in the world: it would suffice to just turn the printing machines on and the whole problems of the world would be solved.

Not only is paper money not money - it is only worth money - but money is not wealth, but only a measure of wealth.

So, what is wealth, then?

Wealth is Production.

It is by the GDP (Gross Domestic Product) that we measure the total production of a country, which is the sum of all wealth generated by its citizens.

Wealth comes from the work of each one of us every single day, from the entrepreneur who starts the process of production to the farmer planting in the field, from the barber who cuts hair, a doctor who consults a patient, a taxi driver who takes a passenger to another place in the city, etc.

Every product or service generated creates wealth.

The only role that money has is to simplify the exchange of these products and services that have been generated. Again: money only simplifies the exchange of wealth. It makes life a lot easier than it was when we were limited to bartering, but it does not create wealth.

In the end, each one of us produces something useful to all and is compensated for that. You receive money that can be exchanged for another good or service that someone else has produced and so on.

The value of money is how much in terms of goods and services you can exchange it for. It is the goods and services that give value to money and not the opposite.

Money, which today is represented by paper money, checks, coins, numbers on a computer screen, etc. has taken many different forms in the past.

One of the earliest currencies in history was food.

It was in ancient Babylon over 4,000 years ago that the first versions of banknotes started to circulate.

Since food was the main currency, the "bank" used to work like this: instead of carrying around a heavy bag of grains, you could simply store your bags of grain in a warehouse and receive in exchange a tablet of clay representing what you had left there - a bit similar to what we do nowadays when we leave a coat or a bag in a museum bag check, getting a small voucher for it. The clay tablets were the vouchers.

Grain sacks were the bargaining chip, except that instead of exchanging the sacks that were stocked in the warehouse, people realized that it would be easier to trade their own clay tablets, streamlining and simplifying trades.

Everyone knew that for every clay tablet there was a sack of grain stored.

And it was that stored bag that gave value to the tablets.

In practice, this is what we call ballast economy.

If you had a lot of tablets in Babylon, you would be rich. You could eat, drink and even wear whatever you wanted. You could even lend clay tablets with compound interest rates!

There was only one problem. As grains that gave value to the tablet rot sooner or later, the clay tablet eventually evolved into something that was more durable and yet rare.

Salt met these requirements.

In a world where refrigerators did not exist yet, salt had enormous intrinsic value. Not only does it not spoil but it doesn't let food spoil.

Moreover, it is divisible into very tiny grains, the equivalent of a few cents today, and consequently, easy to transport. It was also rare because at that time its extraction process was not simple at all.

Everything a currency has to be, salt was: rare, divisible and durable.

The role salt played as a currency was so important that nowadays we still call our payment at the end of the month of "salary" thanks to what the Romans used to receive in the form of salt.

After salt, many other types of currency such as leather, tobacco, cattle, precious metals like copper and gold followed.

Anything that was rare, divisible, and enduring could be used as a currency.

All of them were currencies created and mined by people themselves. That means that they were all private currencies that did not depend on a government for absolutely anything.

It is always good to remind those who believe that bitcoins and other crypto currencies have invented private currencies.

Governments started dealing with currencies only by 600 B.C. in the region where today is Turkey with the purpose of regulating and avoiding monetary frauds related to metals that were fused with other heavier and less valuable ones.

No, currency counterfeiting is not recent.

Today, that banknote that claimed to be worth money is now seen as money itself.

A paper ballot has exchange value simply because everyone accepts it as a bargaining chip. In other words, everyone accepts it just because they believe everyone else will also accept.

It's kind of crazy, I know, but that's just what it is.

It is in this collective trust that paper money sustains the status of money nowadays. And by this reason, it is called fiat currency. But all the rest remains unchanged. The value of a currency remains the total value of the products or services that can be exchanged for it. It has no intrinsic value.

The idea is, with this, to demystify the role of money in the economy.

Some people think that money is the solution to all of their problems. For others, it is the origin of all evil. Keep that in mind forever, money is not an end by itself, only a means. A means of exchange. And this does not diminish its importance in any way.

Rich is not a society that has a lot of money. A rich society is the one that produces valued goods and services. This is what will give value to its currency.

CHAPTER FIVE

Money brings happiness

Another very common excuse is that money doesn't bring happiness.

Bullsh*t!

Have you ever seen anyone at the end of the month, saying, "Just received my paycheck, I am pissed!"?

Certainly not, right? Me neither.

And in the end, it turns into another mental block to financial success.

If money does not bring you happiness, why do you work the whole month to receive it? Why would you exchange your free time, spend less time with your kids, your family and friends for money?

At least money avoids the sadness of not having it.

Of course, money brings happiness, that's one thing. Another completely different is that, despite bringing happiness, money and happiness are not synonymous. You are right, they are not.

There are a lot of wealthy people that are unhappy.

But there are also a lot of healthy people that are not happy. People that have what to eat every day, have a beautiful family, friends, access to good education, with professional achievements and so, and yet they are not happy.

Does that mean that none of these things bring happiness?

Of course, that's not it.

The thing is that happiness is a state of mind that results from a combination of many different things. Just having money is no guarantee for happiness.

And money only brings real happiness when it comes from real achievements. It is incapable of bringing true peace when it comes from illicit or corrupt activities. Or, less serious, but still less rewarding, when it is the result of the efforts of other people, such as the aid of relatives or Government, an inheritance or a gift.

I'm not saying money coming from others is not good. But financial aid is important as a means and not as an end. If you use the help you receive from others to boost yourself to generate your own resources in the future, that is great.

However, if you simply get used to being helped by others all the time, you will surely end up cultivating a bad relationship with money. Money for you will be a synonym of dependence instead of success, being a source of discomfort in your life.

Always try to walk with your own feet. If at any time, for any reason, you receive help, interpret it as an opportunity. It should serve as a stepping stone for you to grow, so that in the future you do not need it anymore.

Money that brings enduring happiness is that which you have conquered in an honest and fair way, the fruits of your effort and your own production.

Some people that receive help from others have a dangerous thought which is "if I work to receive what they are offering me, I will lose the help I receive, so it isn't worth it". But I'll tell you this: it is always better to earn it yourself rather than by taking charity. Believe me, even if the final result of your effort is smaller than the help you would receive.

Being independent is itself a prize. No one will ever be great without first getting rid of small thoughts like that.

Treat money well and it will reward you. Happiness is not a right, but an achievement.

This works with everything in life.

For some reason, we learn that every time we say money is important, we have to match it with a "but it is not everything in life".

By any chance, every time you tell your wife that she is important, do you also say that she is not everything in your life?

"Look, sweetheart, I love you, but there are other things that are more important, okay?"

If you keep saying that to others all the time, you're going to end up pushing them away from you.

With money it is the same thing.

Money is not everything in life. In a hierarchy of importance, it certainly will not be at the top. OK, understood, but now stop repeating this because money might hear it.

CHAPTER SIX

Economy is a win-win game

Let's get back to the discussion whether wealth is a relative concept or not and that perception that the reason why poor people don't have enough is because rich people have a lot. For this thought, wealth is given, it's a limited resource.

If I saw things this way, I would tend to define rich people as naturally mean. Of course, because if the price of having a nice sports car was people having less food in Africa it would be a huge sin to even think about producing such a thing in the first place.

But I don't see things this way. I don't think that the act of not buying a sports car would automatically put food on the table of hungry people. What I see is that my work generates wealth for me and well-being for the customers. Buying a sportscar would then generate for me well-being and wealth for all those somehow related to its production, direct or indirectly. These people would search for their own well-being by buying things they need or want, generating opportunities for all those willing to produce anything of value. And when they do, they will exchange their products for wealth that can be swapped for anything they want.

The way I see the economy is the way I see life and for me, life can only be good if it's good for the people I know, and as good as it can be for the others I don't know. I see no gain in unjustified sufferings. By the way, suffering can only be justified by a high level of joy in the future that is worth that suffering. Other than that, it is just stupid.

It's funny because my wife and I, we don't see it the same way. From time to time we find ourselves in discussions regarding the different way we approach life.

One day we were at the mall and it was raining cats, dogs, monkeys and the entire fauna of Lion King.

Lucky enough, we had no umbrella with us (Damn it, you Subjected guys!). After we'd finished what we had to do, I prepared to go get the car in the outdoor parking. Of course, I didn't want to get wet, but I couldn't see any reasonable way out except to go get the car in the rain. That was it. My wife sympathized with me and decided she would go get the car with me. So, for a rational person, that is the worst possible outcome. I was looking for a way to avoid one person from getting wet and now her suggestion was that 2 people would get wet instead, doubling the rate of the bad result.

I know the example sounds silly even though it's a true story, but it has a deep meaning. For her, it was a way to say: No matter what happens in life I'll be by your side. It's very sweet and by the way, I know she will always be there for me and this is why we got married. But, honestly, her solution was very counterproductive.

The way I prefer to put it is: I'll always be there for you to make our life the best it can be. And only happy people can make others happy.

Do you get excited when you see people who are depressed? When you see people having a hard time in life? Most people will say they don't, but that is not the way they act in life. The way they treat happiness is exactly the same way the see wealth. They act as if happiness and wealth were limited resources. In that sense, sacrificing is justifiable because giving away their well-being should make other people feel better.

I don't enjoy seeing people suffering and I don't like sacrifices, I don't want people to suffer for me and I don't want to suffer for them. I will avoid unjustified suffering of any kind as much as I can. For me, happiness in unlimited and it grows higher when shared. It works like a domino's effect. Only happy people can make others happy. It's a bit like the airplane safety instructions: Put your oxygen mask on yourself first, and then help others. Of course, because if you are unconscious you are not going to be able to help anybody, right? That is my point, be happy first and then, help spread happiness all over. Happiness is a snowball.

And so is wealth.

Have you ever seen anybody getting rich by its own? No, people get rich by employing other people, paying taxes and more than that: They get rich by creating solutions for society's problems. That is what successful entrepreneurs do.

I know people have different perceptions, creed and ways to interpret things. Well, I have mine.

Stephen Covey in his best-selling book "7 Habits of Highly Effective People" divides people's relationships into what he calls the 6 paradigms of human interaction.

1. Win-Win: Both people win. Agreements or solutions are mutually beneficial and satisfying to both parties.

2. Win-Lose: Wins are perceived as better when the other side of the table loses. Win-Lose people are prone to use position, power, credentials, and personality to get their way.

3. Lose-Win: "I lose, you win." Lose-Win people are quick to please and appease and seek strength from popularity or acceptance. They are not so different to the number 2 people because they also see joy as limited resource, but instead they are prone to give the other people win and stay with the "lose" in order to avoid guilty feelings or maybe due to external factors such as their religion.

4. Lose-Lose: Both people lose. When two Win-Lose people get together - that is, when two, determined, stubborn, ego-invested individuals interact - the result will be Lose-Lose. It is also very common among people that see winning as a sin. They don't want to be sinners, so they prefer to get into relationships where there are no gains involved, and, as a result, both are worse in the relationship than they were before.

5. Win: People with the Win mentality don't necessarily want someone else to lose - that's irrelevant. What matters is that they get what they want.

6. Win-Win or No Deal: If you can't reach an agreement that is mutually beneficial, there is no deal.

Do you want to know how I see this book? I see it as the best-selling book that will help hundreds of thousands of people organize their financial lives. I want them to use my Financial Planning Spreadsheet and I want it to be as helpful for them as it has been for me in these last 12 years. I want to read people saying this book helped them change their lives for the better. I want to make people see the world in a different way. When I receive constructive criticism, I will make changes to improve its content. This book is a living piece. If I receive positive feedback, I know I'll be heading the right way to make the change I want to see. And once I'm done with my purpose, I'll also be better off. But the main commitment I have here is with you. Your success will be my success and that is the only way I can see it. It has to be a Win-Win relationship.

But for some people, when you show them clearly that you also think about your own success, people think you're greedy, cheap and so on. Some people simply hate knowing that the other person is also searching for her own benefits. They want to win alone. They want to have book recommendations, but they don't want to buy the book by clicking on your affiliate link because they know if they do so, you will get a percentage of that. Why? Is that person going to save money by not buying through your link? No, they won't because the price won't change. It's just that instead of being grateful for the recommendation you've given; they prefer you don't win anything and neither do they. Now tell me, who is greedy? Who is cheap?

These people don't believe in Win-Win relationships, they are all so focused on the Win-Lose and Win-Only that they end-up finding it all in ruins.

There is no way one can be successful alone. If you think you are going to be worse just because somebody else is going to be better, you are already worse. You won't find any progress in your life until you switch envy feelings into inspiration.

Don't feel resentful for another person's success. Instead, use it as a source of inspiration. Change your thoughts and your energy will change! As a result, the way you see life is also going to change. Everybody's win will affect your world positively.

Think about the economics. When there is a world crisis, what will happen to you? Every one of us have something that we could lose directly or indirectly in an economic crisis, either you're aware of it or not. You can lose your job, a big part of your investments, or at least you lose opportunities. You might be worse off just because many of the commerce you use to be a client of, now had to close.

When other people are worse, we're worse too.

And the opposite is also true. Economic abundance leads to incredible opportunities, higher paying jobs, business deals and so on.

Everything is linked. The simple definition of economy is the Win-Win relationship. People trade where both sides are better off after they make the trade than they were before it, otherwise that trade would never happen.

And the reason why I'm saying all this is not just because I want you just to be nice to other people. I want you to be nice with yourself first. When you form a bad opinion of other people's success, this plays against your own success because you end up thinking that if someday success knocks in your door, it might make other people feel diminished too.

Free yourself from these tiny little thoughts and it will be the best change in your life ever.

CHAPTER SEVEN

Who is in charge of your life?

All these numbers, all knowledge about the investment world, stock markets and so on won't mean anything if the word "accountability" doesn't mean much to you.

All possible changes start with you! And only with you! It doesn't matter how good or bad you think the world is. How fair or unfair it is. Life itself is neutral. We make it beautiful, we make it ugly, life is the energy we bring to it. What matters is how you deal with this world the way it is.

There are three very important characteristics that will allow you to have full control of your economic life: 1) Responsibility and accountability; 2) Willingness to self-develop, and 3) Courage.

Without these 3 main characteristics it will be impossible for you to acquire any peace of mind or success regarding your financial life.

Marisa Urban, consultant at Human Capital, created the concepts of The Subject and The Subjected, two opposed personalities, as a way to show the impacts of these different behaviors.

Below you will find a summary of them:

Subject :

- Takes responsibility
- Is able to give an answer to a situation that he did not cause

- Does not hide behind real excuses
- Focus on the future
- Does not complain
- Does not blame his parents, boss, HR, politicians, the country, the climate, etc.
- Makes it happen
- Focuses on the power of action that he has.

Subjected :

- Does not recognize his responsibilities. It is always someone else's.
- Believes that good excuses can justify his errors (funny enough, this is not always valid for other people).
- Decreases his power of resolution.
- Believes that everything that happens in his life is the fault of others or due to lucky events and circumstances.
- Usually sees himself as unlucky with nothing working out in his life.
- Lives by lamenting things that have occurred in the past.
- Expects things to suddenly just happen in his life.
- Cares too much about blaming.

A classic example of a Subject's mindset is the story of Sir Douglas Bader of the British Royal Air Force (RAF) aviation who lost both legs in a near-fatal accident in 1931. He did not give up and returned to the RAF a few years later without his natural legs and became a national hero during World War II, by defending England from the German invasion, having shot down 22 Nazi aircrafts.

He could have had all the excuses in the world to give up on his goals. Losing both legs is difficult for anyone, especially when your profession requires physical aptitude. And 1930 is not 2020!

But instead of whining, he sought the necessary solutions. With mechanical legs, he returned and earned his place in history.

The Subject's mindset is focused on "what can I do?" regardless of whether it was him that caused the problem or not.

After all, come on, if you see an accident on the street, you help the victim, even if it wasn't you who caused the accident, right? (I really hope you would)

On the other hand, the Subjected is the guy who thinks that nothing that goes wrong in his life is due directly to his own decisions or omissions.

He always blames someone else. And he lives complaining.

The Subjected plays a limited role is his own life. He could say, for example: "I was late because of the traffic jam." By hiding himself behind these real excuses, he will never find definite solutions to the problems.

The Subject thinks "OK, I did not anticipate the traffic jam this time, but from now on, I will always leave home earlier."

The Subjected will continue to arrive late every time there is a traffic jam in his town. The Subject won't.

The traffic that the Subjected faces in the morning, he attributes to his lack of luck. And you can imagine him saying, "Did you see the huge traffic jam this morning?"

"I didn't see it because I came early," would answer the Subject.

"Lucky you!" Would reply the Subjected.

This is a small example, but when you apply it to every attitude in your life it will define where you end up.

I am not saying that we have 100% control of what happens in our lives. We simply don't.

Machiavelli used to say that 50% of what we achieve in life is due to fortune, meaning events that depend on luck. And the other 50% is a virtue, a result of our own choices and attitudes.

I am not sure that this distribution is really 50-50, but what I do know is that even if luck plays an important part, there is a whole other part that is up to us only, and since we cannot control luck, all there is to do is to focus on our zone of attitude.

The main characteristic that defines Subjects and Subjecteds is the way they see things differently. Subjects focus on their power of action. And it doesn't matter if it is 50% of the impacts in his life or only 10%. The thing is that this is the only part of your life that you have control of and, therefore, that is the only part you should focus on!

Everything else is a complete waste of time. You cannot control if it will rain or not, but you can always bring an umbrella. That's the spirit!

We, human beings, are curious creatures. We're quick to accept full credit for our success. When we win, we want to tell the whole world how we made it ourselves.

But we tend to be equally quick to blame external factors for each of our setbacks. Salesmen blame customers, Executives blame employees and employees blame their Managers. When money is short home, husband blames wife and vice versa.

I personally have never seen anyone saying that the main reason for his or her success was the economic growth. It's always a story about how their personal efforts paid them back. Yet, we see millions of people blaming the economic crisis for their setbacks. After all, the economy only plays an important part in failure? This is a typical Subjected way of seeing things.

Subjects are easily identified. The Subjecteds also identify them and either seek to live at their expense or attribute all the achievements of the Subject to luck.

There are people who are typical Subjects, others are complete Subjecteds.

By now, you probably have already identified someone from your family, your work, your circle of friends, etc. There's always someone playing a victim somewhere out there acting as if they were simple voyeurs in their own lives.

It is a lot easier to hide behind external factors that you have no control of. You are not where you wished you would be in your life? It's not your fault, it's your parent's or maybe just a sequence of bad luck…

Hmmm…

This passive attitude will take you nowhere. In some cases, some people fit exactly into the description of either a Subject or Subjected, but most of the time, we all can behave either as one or the other depending on the situation.

People when afraid become weak and some end up acting as Subjected to justify their failures instead of facing them.

Life, to be well lived, has to be faced head on.

This inevitably leads to feelings of gains and losses. The first step to evolve is to take responsibility. Recognize your mistakes, even if it is the one of omission.

If you are in a poor financial situation, focus on what **you** can and must do so that it will change. Stop blaming your company, the taxes, your wife or husband, your parent. I-don't-care! And life doesn't care either. No one's life is perfect.

If you believe that everything wrong that happens in your life is someone else's fault and not yours, you will never do anything to change. As a result, you won't grow.

It's important to admit that as a human being, you're going to make mistakes. We all do. The difference between the Subject and the Subjected is not in how much each one is exposed to the error, but in how they face it.

For the Subject, finding a mistake is seen as a lever for his development. For the Subjected, mistakes are a source of shame. Therefore, he hides these mistakes by trying his best to either justify them with real excuses or blaming somebody else.

A new type of competition

The Mindset of the Subject brings us the idea that life is really with us and that the focus is always on "what can I do?". Consequently, the competition that will matter in your life is between you and yourself.

It doesn't matter if you are currently in a certain financial situation and your neighbor is in another. It doesn't matter if his car is nicer than yours or not.

What matters is where you are within the plan you have set for yourself. You will change your behavior regarding the others. Anyone in your life will be a new source of inspiration and learning that can be used to get you further. Beating yourself is the greatest victory anyone can ever win.

Be thankful!

I thank God every night before going to bed, before every meal and recently I created the habit of cultivating a little grateful notebook where every morning I write things like "I am grateful for having a family or because it's a sunny day".

I always try to add something I have never been thankful for before. It's worth no matter your religion. Buddhist, Muslim, Catholic, Protestant, Jewish... It works even for atheists.

To be thankful is a sign of humility in life. It is a state of mind.

"Riko, did it turn into a self-help book?" Just a little, but the aspect remains the same: The Subject mindset.

The truth is that stopping for a few minutes every day to exercise gratitude will challenge you to seek the positive aspect in everything that happens to you. As a consequence, you will cultivate optimistic habits.

Instinctively, you will see everything that happens in your routine with a different look, always seeking the positive side in everything.

To begin with, optimistic people are more captivating and often attract good things, but in addition to that, when looking for positive things, you will be challenged to always find solutions to any situation no matter how difficult it may seem to be.

You will always be looking for new opportunities and you will only seize opportunities if you are able to first identify them.

In fact, professionally, in my personal life, in everything, I follow a very practical and simple philosophy: focus on the solution, not on the problem.

You have a problem? How helpful can be whining, complaining and finding someone to blame?

The focus is: "how to solve it?". Forget where it came from, who caused it, bla bla bla... Just go and solve it!

If there is no way to solve it, then, you're already all set.

It is better to spend energy on productive things. Once it is solved, looking at the root of the problem will be important to avoid it happening again in the future. But only afterwards. It's a matter of priority.

Before moving on to the next section, I would like to say that there are two types of optimistic people: the "optimistic hands on" and the "lazy optimistic". The former trusts himself, that the things he does will work. The latter expects good things to magically happen in his life, he dreams of winning the lottery or receiving a huge inheritance from someone - sometimes from someone that doesn't even exist - and so on.

In short, the "pessimist" complains about the wind. The "lazy optimist" believes it will change direction. And the "optimistic hands on" adjusts the sails.

Focus on solution, always!

CHAPTER EIGHT

It's more about who you want to be

Being either a Subject or a Subjected are not traits we are born with. We can always change, and the first step is to acknowledge all this.

Most people that stop to think about it for the first time and identify their Subjected behaviors, end up changing them.

Carol Dweck in her book Mindset present us with two other kinds of mindsets that she calls the Growth and the Fixed mindsets.

For anyone that hasn't already read it, basically, a person with a Growth Mindset is the one that believes in change and development. He believes that you are able to turn into whoever you want to be, and you can accomplish the things you value. All is possible with effort and development.

The Fixed Mindset believes that your qualities are carved in stone. So, you were born with certain characteristics that you will carry for your entire life.

This mindset creates an urgency to prove yourself over and over because if you believe you only have a certain amount of intelligence, a certain personality and a certain moral character, you better prove that you have a healthy dose of them.

Most of us are trained in the Fixed Mindset from an early age. People usually try to identify fixed traces of our personality since the very moment we are born and they will be looking for things like: are you smart or not, kind or not, well-educated or not, good in sports or not, and so on… and whatever you don't start already good at, you end up by giving up as if you were "not born for that".

"*It is not his thing*". They'll say.

When people believe in fixed traits, they are always in danger of being measured by a failure because it can define them in a permanent way. For the people with a fixed mindset, they don't just fail, they become the failure.

When people believe their basic qualities can be developed, failures may still hurt, but they will not define them. If abilities can be expanded - if changes and growth are possible - then there are always many paths to success. But that requires effort. A lot of effort, actually.

For the fixed mind, effort is terrifying for two reasons. One is that, for them, great geniuses are not supposed to need it. And the second is that it robs you of all your excuses. I'll get back to this point in the next topic, but the thing is that without effort, you can always say: "I could have been XYZ". But once you tried, you cannot say that anymore. You either have been or not, and if not, for the Fixed Mindset, that means that you would never be.

Fixed mindset people live in a world where some people are superior and some are inferior and, of course, no one wants to be inferior. That is why they are afraid that people might outperform them. So, they are wary of people willing to grow, like new people in their jobs or friends and so on.

True self-confidence is the courage to be open, to welcome change and new ideas regardless of their source. Real self-confidence is not reflected in a title, an expensive suit, a fancy car, etc. It is reflected in your mindset: your readiness to grow.

Leadership is about growth and passion. Not about brilliance. One thing Warren Bennis took from several interviews he had with great leaders was that all of them agreed that leaders are made, not born.

Everyone no matter what age and circumstance is capable of self-transformation. The more you challenge your mind to learn, the more brain cells grow.

Growth Mindset people believe change is possible and desired. They are open to feedback that allows them to see points where they can develop.

Feedback for Fixed Mindset people is always very complicated. As they don't believe in change, they take it all personally. They see no point in all that: they either are praised for their qualities or they will be disappointed at any point that they lack and would need to develop. And they usually react by pointing out the faults of the people that provided the feedback instead of embracing the opportunity to develop something new.

People with the fixed mindset think the world needs to change, not them. They always feel entitled to something better - a better job, a better country, a better house or spouse. The world should recognize their special qualities and treat them accordingly.

In many aspects, the Fixed Mindset looks like the Subjected. They see themselves as gifted, so the only source of problems they face in their lives is due to external factors. Only! It is never their fault.

I am not saying that fixed traits don't play a role in our lives. Again, of course they do, but maybe we tend to believe that natural talent outweighs effort.

In the table below, you will find a list of the Medicine Hat Tigers players, one of the finest teams in the Canadian Hockey League.

Name	Position	Height	Weight	Birth Date	Hometown
Tyler Ennis	C	5'9"	160	Oct 6, 1989	Edmonton
Jordan Hickmott	C	6'	183	Apr 11, 1990	Mission
Jakub Rumpel	RW	5'8"	166	Jan 27, 1987	Hrnciarovce
Bretton Cameron	C	5'11"	168	Jan 26, 1989	Didsbury
Chris Stevens	LW	5'10"	197	Aug 20, 1986	Dawson's Creek
Gord Baldwin	D	6'5"	205	Mar 1, 1987	Winnipeg
David Schlemko	D	6'1"	195	May 7, 1987	Edmonton
Trever Glass	D	6'	190	Jan 22, 1988	Cochrane
Kris Russell	D	5'10"	177	May 2, 1987	Caroline
Michael Sauer	D	6'3"	205	Aug 7, 1987	Sartell
Mark Isherwood	D	6'	183	Jan 31, 1989	Abbotsford
Shayne Brown	D	6'1"	198	Feb 20, 1989	Stony Plain
Jordan Bendfeld	D	6'3"	230	Feb 9, 1988	Leduc
Ryan Holfeld	G	5'11"	166	Jun 29, 1989	LeRoy
Matt Keetley	G	6'2"	189	Apr 27, 1989	Medicine Hat

Can you see it?

No? Try once again and see if you can find a curious pattern.

Well, to be honest, don't feel bad if you can't. For many years no one did. It was until the mid-80s that a Canadian psychologist named Roger Barnsley first drew attention to the relative age issue.

Most of the players in this list were born in January, February and March. There is only one player born in October and no one from November or December.

Having realized this, Roger Barnsley searched all Hockey Players to check this pattern. In every elite group of hockey players - the very best of the best - 40% of the players will have been born in January, February and March and only 10% in October, November and December.

The explanation for this is very simple and has nothing to do with astrology. It is just that in Canada, the eligibility cutoff for age-class hockey is January 1. It means that a boy born on January 1 could play the rest of the year with someone born on December 31 - even if he is 12 months older than the younger players.

It is an amazing advantage in the early ages! He is not only more developed physically but also more mature.

Malcolm Gladwell in his great book Outliers showed us lots of examples following this pattern around the globe, in addition to the one above.

Sports is a good example because it is a field where most people believe that you have to be born with natural talent. The hockey list was the starting point since the psychologist who discovered it was Canadian, but the pattern doesn't change in soccer, football, basketball... More than that, we even see this happening in school and other everyday activities!

Think about that, all these boys are being judged by their results while playing in very different conditions. For the ones raised in a Fixed Mindset culture, this will most likely be the end of the game for most of them. If they don't do well in the early ages, they will just give up believing they were not born for that.

But the same research concluded that what was key for the different development was practice. When you are 10 or 12, a 12 months difference in age is very high, but once you grow up, this physical and mental gap narrows. When you are 17, it won't matter that much anymore. But by then, it will be too late for most of these kids. Some of them will have simply given up. For the ones that persist, they will do so in different conditions. When you outperform in the early ages, you get to be selected to regional and national teams. There, you get to practice a lot more in more structured conditions and high-level environment - an advantage that will be hard to catch up for those who did not have the same opportunities.

What I want to say with all this is that practice plays a more important and definite role in our achievements than fixed traits, even if sometimes it is not so obvious to realize it.

Practice is not the thing you do since you are good. It is the thing you do that makes you good.

Once you realize it and start acting as a Growth Mindset Subject, whatever your goals are, they will always be possible.

CHAPTER NINE

Brave vs. Genius

Another type of personality we often see around is what I call the "pseudo-genius".

You must have known someone like this, considered by all an outlier without ever having gotten good grades at school or studied at good universities, or had good jobs, nor has he ever been interested in starting a business or made any great achievement, but the rare small things he could do with perfection.

They are the "what if..."s. They live by feeding a collective fantasy making everyone around them believe that they could succeed in whatever they want and that they just do not do it because they don't want to.

And they don't want anything.

They hide themselves fearing not being able to achieve what is expected from them. They prefer to avoid challenges in order to not disappoint those who consider them as superheroes.

The question is: do you prefer to be brave or a genius?

Being intelligent is not necessarily the opposite of being brave, but when you have courage, the fantasy of intelligence as a super-power eventually falls. Because unlike the "pseudo-genius", the brave puts himself in check, he tests himself and deliberately decides to face some situations where he will rarely get through without any setbacks.

The brave is willing to try and if necessary, lose battles.

It is the legitimate "let's go for it" type of person!

The brave is willing to learn and try again with courage and the virtue of not giving up no matter what happens.

The brave fears but overcomes his fear.

It is the typical boy who got good grades at school, relegated to a less noble class of student recognized as "just hard workers".

Only that he is THE man.

It is likely that he has made a commitment to attend the best colleges, get good jobs even if through difficult days, sleepless nights, feelings of failure, and having almost given up several times.

In everything, he learned. Overcoming it all, what is his best characteristic.

This is the great man, the one of great achievements.

Ironically in the end, with his success, it is highly probable that from afar people would still say "See that guy? He has always been an outlier."

If he listened to it, he would be proud to respond: "Not at all, I'm just someone that puts in a lot of effort!"

Because it is better to be brave in life than to cultivate a fanciful image. Nothing can be worse than getting old and hear the comment: "So smart, he had all the potential to be successful." Because what matters the most in life is our attitude. Much more than any subjective quality that people by convention end up giving to some people.

I say: if you have to choose between maintaining an intelligent status or being brave, choose the second one!

Go for it!

Are you the best student in your class? Change your classroom!

Always seek higher goals!

Failures are just a part of the game, but a Subject Mindset will make you learn from each fall and the result will lead to amazing growth.

To conclude this section, I reproduce here an excerpt of the speech made by Theodore Roosevelt at the University of Sorbonne in Paris in 1910.

It has to do with everything I say in this chapter. I read it every time I need to make an important decision in my life. It makes me feel good and encourages me to go to the arena!

It is not the critic who counts; Not the man who points out how the strong man stumbles, or where the doer of deeds could have done them better. The credit belongs to the man who is actually in the arena, whose face is marred by dust and sweat and blood; who strives valiantly; who errs, who comes short again and again, because there is no effort without error and shortcoming; but who does actually strive to do the deeds; who knows great enthusiasms, the great devotions; who spends himself in a worthy cause; who at the best knows in the end the triumph of high achievement, and who at the worst, if he fails, at least fails while daring greatly, so that his place shall never be with those cold and timid souls who neither know victory nor defeat.

CHAPTER TEN

The triad of value: time, money and energy

There are three main things you'll need in your life to accomplish whatever you set as a goal: time, money and energy.

I know we just had this discussion about monkeys, monsters and boxes and some people say time is the most valuable asset you have because it is the scarcest. But I personally think that all 3 are equally valuable. At least, potentially. What will give each of them a higher score is exactly its scarcity in your life. Try to ask a hungry kid what is the most valuable out of the 3, but don't expect her to answer that it's time.

Time and Money are both linked to our most primitive instinct that is the one of survival. People tend to think of money as that piece of paper, but remember, money is not the synonym of cash.

As we said earlier, that piece of paper symbolizes production, and we all need a certain portion of constant production in order to survive. Remember this: if the fish that is feeding you was not fished by you, somebody else did it for you. There is no such thing as a free lunch. And no one in this entire world could live only by free time lying in a hammock or writing poems to the loved ones. Production is a need – and therefore – money is a need!

Every day we wake up is a new day with new necessities: food that keeps us alive is the most obvious, but then you have to dress yourself to protect against the cold weather (or the warm), you'll need a place to sleep, you'll need social interactions, etc.

Production is as important as time. The key in this equation is to find the perfect balance between them. The more you have of one, the more the other will be valuable.

Someone unemployed has all free time of the world and all he is probably looking for is an occupation that will enable him to meet at least his basic needs.

Busy people will try to do their best to optimize their time.

Scarcity will define which one is more valuable, but ultimately both are very, very important and can't be denied by anyone. So, have you ever stopped to think about how much your time is worth? If not, do it now: what is your current situation? Which one do you think is currently more important to you? Time or Money?

I know... we all wished days were longer and that we could also have more money. We all do. But "both" is not an option.

The most practical way of thinking about it is to question yourself: if you received a reasonable offer to work some extra hours of your current free time, would you accept it?

Now, think about it another way. Imagine it was a real possibility: would you pay your employer to have some more free time? If yes, how much would you be willing to pay him by hour? The same amount you earn by hour or a higher one (well, it can be lower, right?)?

So, if the first question was an easier "yes" for you, it means money is more valuable right now in your life. If "yes" was the second option's answer, time is more valuable to you, especially if you said you're in a position to pay more for free time than what you receive per hour.

Let me put it this way: are you in debt or are you an investor? Because for the first one, money is scarce and therefore, they are making their time less valuable. The second one is actually buying free time in the future. Time is more valuable for investors.

As it is the level of scarcity that will give value to any kind of asset, people in debt cannot say they would be willing to buy free time because money is short for them. How could you buy free time if you have no money?

Think about it for a while. Over consuming doesn't mean "you don't care that much about money". Instead it says, "you don't care that much about your time".

Ultimately, Financial Planning is about using money to make your time more valuable.

As money is the main subject of the book, I'll talk about the other two main limited elements you should make good use of to achieve the best results.

Time

Even if somehow subjective, measuring the value of your time is very important. Let's go back to our 2 questions: are you currently more likely to exchange time for money or money to time? And at what rate?

For the ones that picked money: what is the minimum you would accept to be paid for one extra hour of work?

For the ones that chose time: what is the maximum you would accept to pay for one additional free hour?

Think about it for a moment and come with your number! You just have to answer one of the two questions, the one that suits you better.

For the ones that wouldn't be willing to neither sell nor buy extra time, your number is the amount per hour you currently make at your job.

For the salaried ones, all you have to do is divide your salary by the number of hours you usually work.

Now that all of you have your own number, keep it in mind. It will tell you how much an additional portion of your time is valued.

The value of time

One day has 24 hours, that's it! Nothing I know is more democratic and just as time is. We all have the same amount of time in a day no matter if you're a student in 8th grade or if you are Bill Gates.

Yet, countless people think and act like they are the busiest person on the planet even if they are not successful at all. If that is the case, man, I'm sorry to tell you, but you are using your time in a very poor way. You have to be more productive. And the good news is that you can! Everybody can, even Mr. Gates can.

The difference between successful people and ordinary ones is that the former is always looking for ways to find a more productive use of time, either in his professional life or in the time spent with family and friends.

The value of your time is the value you will give to it.

MJ de Marco in the Millionaire Fastlane wrote about it using the example of a long line he once saw for a free bucket of chicken and I think it illustrates very well my message here.

"Why will most people never get rich? Look no further than a $6 bucket of chicken. It made big news: a major fast food restaurant offered a free bucket of chicken to anyone who had

an Internet coupon. People flocked to restaurant locations and waited for hours, all for a free $6 bucket of chicken.

These stories are common and yet my reaction is the same: what the hell is wrong with people? I'll tell you what is wrong with them: these people value their time at zero. It's free. Like the air we breathe, they believe their time is abundant and in endless supply. They live as if they were immortal. They are certain that time, the fuel of their lives, never run empty.

I wonder if these people had three weeks left to live, would they be standing in line for a bucket of chicken? What if they had three months? Three years? At what mortal threshold would logic and reason smack sense into people? And affirm that waiting three hours for a free bucket of chicken is not time well spent? The greasy chicken truth: Value your time poorly and you will be poor. When time is wasted as a lifestyle choice you will be stranded in places you don't want to be.

Take a look around: how do your friends, family and peers value their time? Are they standing in line to save four bucks? Are they driving 40 minutes to save 10 dollars? Are they parked on the sofa anxiously waiting to see who wins Dancing with the Stars?

The average American watches more than 4 hours of TV each day. In a 65-year life, that person will have spent nine years glued to the tube. Nine years!

Why?

Simple.

Life sucks. Life needs an escape. Life is no good. No plans, no goals, no deadlines...

Show me someone who spends hours online playing Clash of Clans or Candy Crush and I'll show you someone who is probably not very successful. When life sucks, escapes are sought. The more you escape from your own life, the more it will suck."

Long life to the Instant Gratification Monkey!

Only that you can and should stop it before all is gone!

Stop right now wasting your time in living other people's lives in Instagram for hours and hours, watching youtubers doing nothing constructive for hours…

If you are this kind of guy, listen to me right now: simply stop it! What is gone is gone. The Past is over, there is no way back, but there is a whole new future starting in the next second. Change it! No one can go back in time and make a new beginning, but you can start now and make a new end for your life.

Value your time correctly. Know it by heart. What is the value of it right now: $10, $30, $100, $500? If you say $30, don't spend half an hour to save less than $15!

You have to measure it.

It doesn't make sense to pick a 10 minutes line to save $5. This is what is called the Opportunity Cost of your time. Always use it to assess "am I making a good use of my time?".

Same thing for Instagramers, would you be willing to pay $30 to watch somebody else living? I would rather go take a walk in a nice park, go to the beach or hang out with my real friends. Nothing is wrong with a healthy use of social media, but spending your entire life passively watching somebody else live?! Really? And wasting energy discussing politics with no intention to change your mind? What's the point? What's wrong with people??

Be time-value conscious in order to make good decisions. You might have to start now with a lower value for your time but look to the future and commit to make your minutes more valuable each day.

Be more productive in your work, don't procrastinate, control your use of social media, TV... have full control of your financial situation and your time will be worth more.

You are not going to die tomorrow, and likely it won't be in the next three weeks, three months or three years but the truth is we sure won't last forever.

There is no excuse for letting the monkey in to enjoy whatever you have not yet created. It's time to produce, organize and balance it all with conquered joy. Spend the time that has been gained via smart production, never at the expense of others. If you're living on the Government aid, your parents' or you are in debt, sorry to say: your time will not have much value until you conquer your independence.

Not having time is a typical Subjected excuse. It is the same as not having enough money, they all come from the same root problem: you need to manage them in a smarter way. You are the one responsible for that.

Money will give more value to your time.

Tim Ferriss described it best in the 4-Hour-Workweek: Lack of time is actually lack of priority. Once you know what you really want and commit to it, you'll be able to prioritize your time to meet your goals.

Only people that know what they want can say no to what they don't want.

Being productive is completely different from being busy. Most people I know feel they have to occupy their free time with some kind of activity. They do not accept that they could have free time, so they fill it with very stupid things that they will swear are needed.

The irony is that the busier a person is, the more unproductive she is. Being busy in fact is a form of laziness, lazy thinking and indiscriminate action.

The most unproductive people I know are the ones that are always busy. It seems to me that it is the way they found to try to defend their unproductive position. As they know their outcome is poor, they try to compensate that with simple effort and use it as an excuse for their friends, family and bosses: "how dare you say my work is poor since I have been giving so much?"

And the worst is that very often it works.

In reality, what a business really needs is a good final result. It doesn't matter if it took you 5 minutes or 5 days. You should always ask yourself: what is the real importance of what I am currently doing?

Don't get me wrong, effort when used correctly is a great fuel. It's that waste of energy that bothers me. And it brings us to the next pillar.

Energy

I could call it focus or vibration, effort or passion, maybe attention or everything altogether, that is what I mean by energy.

You should keep at the best and highest level.

We all go through ups and downs in our lives, but some of the downs can easily be avoided.

Ea-si-ly. I'll give you a personal example.

I had just moved to another job and I was spending 3 hours of my day commuting to work every day. At the same time, my mind was exploding with great ideas I wanted to implement for the business and for my personal life. I was 100% in the construction mode! My focus was on how I could make things work better and what should I do to improve every single area of my life. We had just moved to a beautiful city full of cool things to see and do, with a 2-year-old baby girl and a 17-year-old teenager and working long hours seven days a week.

My wife was with me, facing the exact same issues. But, for 2 weeks she wasted a bundle of good energy and time just because she couldn't pay her cell phone bill of 20 euros! For weeks, that was the biggest problem of her life! Honestly, thank God because if your worst problem is not finding a way to pay a 20 euros bill, that means your life is doing great!

But still, the point is that it would be even better if she filtered and enjoyed the good moment she was living.

We all do that every now and then, we waste our good energy by giving too much attention to unimportant things while we have a tsunami of reasons to feel thankful for.

Your energy when used correctly is an accelerator for your achievements. Focus on your life, on good things. Use it to decide what you want to achieve in your life and what you should do to get there.

Don't envy people, don't spend time criticizing other people's lives and choices. Learn from them what you can, instead. Saying bad things about other people will lower your energy, will make you weaker and less focused on your goals.

And don't waste your energy with unimportant things. It's not only your time, but also your energy, your focus. Next time you have a problem, step back for a while and think "how big is this problem?".

We tend to overvalue small issues as if we would not be able to get along without them. Don't dramatize! If you were in the death row, would they still matter? So, stop acting if that was the case. Just slow down and remember this: most things make no difference. Either it is a problem you have or a busy task that is meaningless. A lot of people spend a huge amount of energy and time on things that are really not worth.

A good thing I learned from the French people is that they usually think "people are not going to die, and the world won't stop turning if one task is not completed on time". When you apply this way of thinking, surprisingly, you'll finish most of the important tasks you have to do earlier and easier.

The trick here is that, the French people I know focus more on the importance of the task rather than on its urgency. And a lot of urgent things we get solved are not really that important.

But because we have deadlines, we tend to focus on them rather than on the important ones that have no deadlines. We simply react to the Panic Monster when he shows up. And guess what, his motive is simply not the best. If we simply prioritize urgency over importance, we'll focus on unimportant things with deadlines and we'll miss the timing for the important thing just because they don't come with a "due date". Next thing you know your energy is low just because you missed the payment of a 20 euros bill.

Ultimately, we human beings work like those characters in video games with a certain limited amount of stamina. We all are, but we can focus our energy on what will bring us the best results. And now I'm not talking only about your financial life, but in all the different aspects of it.

Sometimes I hear people defending one should go to work through a different road or make different things just to get his or her brain trained. Are you one of these people? please don't be that guy because this can be a huge source of waste of energy.

In his great book Power of Habit, Charles Duhigg shows us how impactful habits are in our brains in a point that once an activity has become a habit, we can perform it with a very low level of effort.

Every great performer in every field has put a lot of time on practicing the activity they excel. Repetition transforms the activity into a habit of making you request from your body and brain decreasing additional levels of energy to perform it. And most things we do can be transformed into habits, such as exercising, reading, studying, planning your financial life, investing, saving, etc. In the beginning, these activities will request a high level of energy, but if you keep performing them for a while, they'll become natural for you and you'll be able to move your focus to something else.

So, if you have enough energy to be used on changing your routines so that you feel your brain is being used, please spare it and focus on the creation of more productive activities such as Budgeting and Investing. Your brain will be trained too, but you are also going to see positive results of this change forever.

In short, spend the least energy as you possibly can in activities that won't lead you to any relevant result and maximize your focus on the ones that will bring you life-changing results. Once controlling your financial life has turned into a habit, it will change your life forever.

Another important aspect is that when we stress about the many things we still have to do; we usually overvalue them. The stress itself is a huge waste of energy that could be used more productively if we had just concentrated on producing and delivering.

Value your time and your energy! Use them always in a constructive way.

Practice it as an exercise and remember that.

CHAPTER ELEVEN

Knowing your "economic self"

Even if you have the Subject attitude towards life, you may still fall in some economic traps that can undermine your entire financial life.

It is important to get to know your "economic self".

There is a theory that says that individuals always behave rationally.

This rationality would work in such a way that our decisions would always seek to maximize our well-being with the least possible effort as if we were always practicing a sort of cost-benefit analysis.

The only problem is that this is not true. At least not all the time.

We are not always able to make the most beneficial decisions for ourselves because most of the time we're led by wrong perceptions.

One of the main roles of Marketing and Sales professionals is to try to figure out the point that they can maximize the profits of their companies simply through the way products are presented.

In that sense, very often, consumers are driven to buy something they did not need or want, and yet leave with the impression of getting a great deal. The promotion of something being sold for $500 when the previous price was $1,500 is meant to give us the feeling that we are saving $1,000 when in fact we are still just spending the $500.

(Just by the way, keep in mind that if you don't buy anything, the discount is higher!)

The trap of relative mentality

The paradox of the pen and the suit is a good example that shows how our brain is able to play tricks on us.

Tversky and Kahneman conducted a study testing the reaction of people in two different situations.

In the first, individuals needed to buy a pen that was sold for $16 at the store next door. The, they were told that they could find the same pen for $1 at a store just a few blocks away - a 15-minute walk.

In the second situation, in a store, when trying a suit that costs $ 500, individuals would find out that the same suit was on sale for $ 485 at another store, also 15 minutes away.

Now, take your time and think about this: what would you actually do in both cases?

The result of the study showed that the majority of people preferred to buy the cheaper pen and spend the $500 in the most expensive suit.

In general, people walk to buy the pen, but not the suit, even though in both cases the gain is the same.

After all, a 15-minute walk is worth $15 or not?

Addiction to the standard of living

The standard of living is addictive. The neighborhood where we live, the restaurants we go to, the trips we take on vacation and the clothes we wear, they all become habits that become part of our daily lives.

Let's take the example of smoking to illustrate this addiction, raising the standard of living is as easy as going back to smoking. Reducing it is as hard as quitting smoking.

Anyone who has ever smoked and at least tried to quit knows what I'm talking about. A lapse of control and you end up a slave to your standard of living.

You wake up early every day and come back late from work to maintain a life that doesn't even bring you that much pleasure, but you just can't let go.

You now earn the amount of money you once have dreamed of earning, but now it seems to you that it is not enough.

Then you blame inflation, not realizing that now you have dinner in nice restaurants and that the beers you drink now are either handmade or imported.

And then it comes the moment where the financial situation gets more complicated and expensive habits that you didn't even know you had are killing any chance you have of building a better future.

The question is: how to change habits then?

People believe that it is not possible. That's the first reaction.

"Nice to haves" become "needs".

How about moving to a cheaper neighborhood? You sit down, do the math and try to convince yourself that even financially it doesn't pay. Sacrifice is a lot higher than the potential savings.

And then your financial life sinks. I repeat, it will be as hard and painful as quit smoking. But it is possible to change.

Many people have no idea of the power of habit and how it is created almost imperceptibly. When you realize it, it's already there. The best you can do is to not create habits that you are not sure you will be able to afford in the long run.

Sometimes I think, "It's only 10 dollars, and you know, $10 is not going to make me any richer or poorer."

True, 10 dollars today wouldn't change my life. But do you guys know how often I think that? Hell! If every time I thought about it, I decided to spend it, then it would certainly change my life. And starts with $10, then turns into $20, $50... Come on, it costs just one hundred dollars!

So, understand this: expenses end up perpetuating.

Paying $5 once for a donut I can, but I cannot do this every day.

So before buying the first $5 donut, I wonder if that's really an atypical situation or a potential new habit.

The "just this once" thought is a huuuge risk.

And what is even worse is that people often use bad spending in the past to justify even worse spending in the future.

You've probably said something like "oh I have spent money on so many unimportant things" to justify an expense that should not be made in the present.

That means: since you've spent so much and so poorly in the past, keep spending it the same way today!

Bad expenses in the past turn into justification of bad expenses in the future. Be aware of that! It's a dangerous vicious circle.

So, every expense counts! Vigilance is always necessary.

On the other hand, if you give up a "good opportunity" in your quest for a balanced financial life, this will serve as a good justification for not wasting money in the future.

You'll think "I gave up a good opportunity like that, I will not waste it now with this."

People in general have no idea of how much spending becomes a habit that is difficult to change later.

Our standard of living becomes a painful need and extremely difficult to change in the short term.

Therefore, before increasing your standard of living, think about it. Assess whether it is something that you can maintain in a healthy and sustainable way because having to lower it back in the future will cause you a greater loss in terms of welfare than the benefit of going one step up in your living standards.

Create good habits. Spending is a habit, but also is saving.

The problem is the "it's only this time". Usually it ruins everything.

Maslow's Pyramid

We tend to overestimate our needs while underestimating our possibilities. We think we need more than we actually do, and we think we can reach less than we actually can. To organize your life, you must have clear in your mind the difference between your needs and your possibilities.

The Maslow's Pyramid is a way of showing hierarchically the necessary conditions for each human being to attain personal and professional satisfaction.

It starts from the physiological needs as the basis of the pyramid such as food, health, water and sleep. Then comes the safety needs, followed by social belonging, self-esteem and finally, at the top of the pyramid, are the needs of self-actualization, when the individual can seize the full potential of himself, with self-control of his actions, independence and ability to do what he loves to do.

Later in the book, we'll go into more details on how to use this concept to organize your investment strategy.

Different consumption profiles

"He says he's broke, but he's always traveling."

"She says she has no money to travel with us, but she's always having dinner out."

"They said they are in a difficult situation, but just bought a new car."

"He says he's broke but living in this nice neighborhood."

"She says she's broke, but she only wears fancy clothes."

You probably have heard comments like these and come on you probably also made some of them at some point.

We human beings we like to judge, that is just the way we are. In our view anyone in a particular situation may seem to be untrue to say that she is out of money when to her, she is just speaking the truth. What justifies this behavior are the different patterns of consumption.

Each one of us has a personality as a consumer that is unique. Some people like to travel more, others eat out, some have a preference to cars, others dream of having a nice house with a swimming pool, others give more importance to location rather than size... well, there are many differences.

So, when one of your friends says that she would like to go to that fancy restaurant, but she can't because she is out of money, her statement could be both a truth and a lie at the same time. It's true at the point where she really might want to go if she had more money. The "lying" part of the story is that it is not that she doesn't have money to go. The point is that it is not a priority for her. With the amount of money, she currently has, it's not worth spending it there.

Before that, she plans to do many other things with her money.

That's because money is a limited resource and each of us has a different ranking of priorities.

And it's not just about consumption. Time is also a very important item in this equation.

So, not everyone will find satisfaction in a professional life considered by others to be successful. Some may think that spending a lifetime selling coconut on the beach is boring. Others will think that of someone who works from 9 to 5 in an office. That is why we have different remunerations for different professions.

Supply and demand, it's as simple as that.

And even if you prefer to eat at restaurants rather than buying clothes, at some point you will have to stop eating out a little bit to replace some garment in the wardrobe. And vice versa.

Because even our preferences are changeable. It changes according to our possessions.

Realizing the existence of these different consumer profiles and knowing that even these profiles are changeable, is essential to plan your own financial life.

Self-knowledge is important for making the best decisions.

And also - why not? - to better understand and respect the different decisions that others make.

Don't judge people by your preferences because they have their own. This can also stop us from depriving others of maximizing their satisfaction just because we do not understand or disagree with them.

Watch out for these "opportunities"!

One of the biggest risks to our financial control is when we face "good opportunities." I know, it may sound like a contradiction, but it is not. An opportunity has 2 sides, one healthy and one not good at all.

What I call an opportunity is a Black Friday promotion of a nice car or trip, or the chance of buying something you always wanted for an incredible price.

There are so many opportunities that arise in our day to day life and there will always be, but to seize an opportunity, you must first be prepared for it. If you are in a moment of organizing your finances, you need discipline before all.

As the Chinese proverb goes "If you can't, well, then you simply can't." (alright, it is not a Chinese proverb, I just invented it. But even if it doesn't sound profound, it is actually very meaningful.)

But it means that being disciplined often requires letting some "good opportunities" go away. The opportunity may be excellent, but not for you at that particular moment. Structure yourself first.

Always think in relative terms.

"Expensive" and "cheap" are relative concepts after all. A trip to a Caribbean island for a thousand dollars can be tempting. But if all you have is that one thousand dollars, that means using everything you have: 100%! It is absurd!

On the other hand, for those who have a reserve of $200,000, paying a most common price of $2,000 for the same trip may seem unfavorable, right? After all, she will be paying double the price of the promotion. But it is only 1% of what she has!

Think of "cheap" in terms of the total cost of what you want to buy over the total you have. And the difference between the first and the second case is that the second person, to get where she is now, she certainly had to give up lots of "good opportunities."

Sometimes - or maybe most of the times - the best thing is to just let these "opportunities" go by. If you have discipline, you will be ready to take advantage of others in the future. And even if they don't exist in the same way in the future, don't worry. Maybe you will not even need them anymore.

Another important thing is that before you buy anything, unless you have left home just to buy it, never do it on impulse. I always wait for a day to think if I really want or need it or if I'm just acting on impulse. If in the next day, I still want it, I go back to the store and buy it, but most of the time, I confess that I just let it go.

You can choose to always be around with a messy budget, fighting the temptations or heading with focus to the top of the financial hill. From above, everything will look smaller and the opportunities will be much greater. And by the way, they will be real opportunities.

Prize for self-control

Keeping control of these temptations is not always easy, but this is what people with financial success do.

A well-known study by psychologist Michael Mischel, a professor from Stanford, showed that children who have been able to resist the temptation to eat a marshmallow for a bigger reward in the future were more likely to develop a successful career than the impatient ones.

It's the famous Marshmallow test.

To analyze the effects of self-discipline, in the 60s, he selected a group of American preschool children and left each kid alone in a room and before leaving it, Mischel offered a marshmallow to each child with a clear rule: the kids should wait for him without eating the candy.

If the kid did not give in to temptation, he or she would win as a prize another candy.

The game turned into a torture for most of the children and only a third managed to wait about 20 minutes for the return of the researcher.

Some years later, in 1981, the difference between the rushers and those who managed to control themselves was blatant. The more patients presented a more positive posture during adolescence. They were more motivated, persistent in difficult situations and were able to delay some reward in favor of their long-term goals.

Children who managed to wait 20 minutes to eat two marshmallows had a greater professional and financial success than those who ate the first candy in a few minutes.

The same applies to every consumption temptation.

CHAPTER TWELVE

Finance in Couples

Money is a smart guy and its greatest charm is its ability to avoid being seen as the villain no matter what the situation. For most couples, the roots of many of their relationship's problems begin with money. Or better said: lack of money.

Difficulties resulting from bad money management often cause problems which the couple doesn't even realize they are financial in nature. If there is no money for a romantic dinner, the perceived problem is lack of romance; if there is no money for clothing, the perceived problem is negligence; if there is no money to take the kids to a theme park, the perceived problem is lack of affection; if there is no money for a cool and adventurous trip in Southwest Asia; the perceived problem is that their marriage has fallen into a boring routine.

Couples rarely have the perception of how much of their relationship problems are caused by poor money management or lack of ability to make ends meet in a healthy way.

The problem is that couples don't talk enough about money proactively but rather after the situation is already out of control.

When it comes to money, people seek help when they are already in trouble and when fixing the problem is much harder, more expensive and a lot more painful.

Sometimes when they realize there is a problem it is too late to save the marriage. After all, money problems are one of the main reasons for divorce. Even when the couple doesn't realize it right away. There is very often financial roots hidden in every story.

Talking about money is good but arguing about money is the symptom that you guys have missed something in the past.

I know, it is always the other person's fault.

But, honestly, blaming is not going to make things any better. There is still time to change and it's better if you perform these changes together.

I lived in that kind of situation with my beloved wife at the time she was still my girlfriend, and we had very different ways of treating money.

As an economist working with the Stock Market, I have always been very money cautious while she... well, let's say "not that much". I had ambitious plans at that time, and I knew we were not going to make them happen if we kept spending time and money as if we were going to die the next day.

So, what I did for several weeks was to discuss a lot about the future. I presented my plans for the future to her and I listened to everything she had to say about them, so that we could turn my plans and her plans into our plans.

Putting it this way makes it look easy and fun, but OMG… in reality, it turned our lives into the Ultimate Fight Championship.

I rarely have a chance to win any fight against her. That's why I am using this book as my silent revenge (I know she won't be able to reply). Anyway, what I want to say is that the planning fight was totally valuable! I know how hard it was for her too. But it's better to be hard in the planning than in the middle of the path, when there is no way back.

The way I see things is that a couple's life when is planned and is goal oriented is happier. It is not always easy; the other person will not always be eager to listen nor share and sometimes your plans simply don't match. But you still need to talk. You need to share your thoughts and plans and little by little, if you are both really open, you'll realize you have a lot more in common than you thought after the first few conversations.

This book is a guide for changing your financial life and the way you treat money. Share this book with your wife or husband or boyfriend etc. Make sure you both are with the same mindset. Try to construct a budget together and make sure both of you participate in the couple's financial lives. This is an important part of making plans together. Commit and support each other to pay the expenses as they have been budgeted. See it as your path to achieving your goals and making you stronger as a couple.

What I see is that usually one is responsible for the finances, while the other usually shows some aversion to numbers. Very honestly, I don't believe there is a magic way that would fit every couple on earth, but I suggest that even if one in the couple is more skillful with numbers than the other, it is still important that they both participate somehow, so that they are both aware of the couple's financial situation. And rather earlier than later.

Math doesn't lie. 1+1 is always going to equal 2, no matter how hard you want to overspend and neglect your budget.

If you don't respect your budget today – I won't lie - the next day you are going to feel as if nothing had changed. If you focus on the short term only, you might have the impression that not respecting your budget is just fine.

But if you fast forward in a month or a year, ends won't meet, and you are going to be either out of cash or in debt. There is no magic. And by the time you realize you're in trouble, it might be too late. Divorce could knock on your door and find you locked in a room blaming your partner for it, depressed, not realizing that the reason for all that mess was a poor financial management.

But you can start changing that reality today...

CHAPTER THIRTEEN

Planning is deciding and committing

A common mistake among the financial controls and spreadsheets out there is that some of them don't include a Budget. Many families simply write down all their day-to-day spending which is a good start, but definitely not enough.

Budgeting is not a guessing game. It is a compromise. It's your commitment to create the future you want for you.

You have to be realistic, for sure, but you can also push a little to challenge yourself. If the result of your realistic forecasting is not in line with your expectations, it means you need to re-think what you're doing.

This is where the importance of budgeting comes in. It will, in the first place, be an exercise of thinking about your future and deciding what you want. Note that I'm using the word "decide" rather than "find out".

Forget about finding out what you want. You'll never find that out because we, human beings, want so many different things at different times that it is almost impossible to think about reaching a point where we don't want anything else.

You have to weigh all the possibilities and choose the ones you want better and commit to them.

If your objective is to work in an investment bank, you'll probably not be able to do so and live in a quiet and isolated Caribbean island at the same time.

It is possible to retire at the age of 50, but if your goal is to visit the maximum of countries in the world before you turn 30, maybe the 2 goals will be difficult to coexist.

That is why it is extremely important to decide what you really want. It is an exercise of organizing ideas.

The risk is to find yourself unhappy when meeting a goal by not identifying it was you who chose it. Or even worse, make your life a story of comings and goings, finding yourself always back to the same place.

Seneca wisely said that "when a man does not know what harbor he is making for, no wind can never be the right wind"

You have to know what harbor you are making for! Don't discover one, decide on one! It is necessary to put on paper your desires, to reflect on its pros and cons. Some of them will be turned into goals and you will commit to them.

It changes everything.

It is when you leave a world in which you do not decide anything for one in which you are the boss! In this process of turning desire into goals, you will end up getting better organized, seeing things more clearly.

When you plan, everything becomes clearer. So, it's worth taking some time for reflection, deciding which way you want to go in your life. Goals such as marrying, having children, buying a property, retiring before 60, changing professions, starting a business, living abroad, learning a foreign language, etc.

Some may be exclusive, so you should be selective.

For me, the best start is to really think about it that way: at the age of 90, looking back, what will you be proud of having done and what will you regret not having done?

Your future will be a step in some direction. It's better that it's in the right one.

But you can only know it if you know the way. It is impossible to achieve an objective that never existed.

Once the objectives and long-term plans are defined, it is up to you to choose the path to get there. Your budget should reflect all that. It is a numbered translation of your path.

If you want to have your honeymoon in Tahiti, the value of the trip should be budgeted. If you do that and respect your Budget, it will come true.

The future is not foreseen, it is built.

CHAPTER FOURTEEN

Control your Finance

Most people believe that good mental financial control is enough. From time to time they check their bank accounts to take a look at the balance, look at the credit card balance every month and sometimes swear that a certain amount that has been charged was not due simply because - as human beings we all are - they don't remember everything they spent money on.

It happens to everyone who acts this way. We don't manage what we don't control. It is important to keep full control over everything that comes in and out of your financial life. You need to know exactly where you are!

With the information in hand, you will be able to analyze your financial life, make the right decisions and choose what has to be changed.

I was 19 when I started to live by myself and take control of my financial life. Just before moving away from my parents' house, I remember writing down in a notebook what my budget would be from then on. It included the cost of rent, groceries, energy, etc. All regular monthly expenses. But in that budget, there was no room for going out for a beer with friends or buying clothes for example.

I learned a lot there. I started to freak out as soon as I started to do the math and I couldn't reach a positive balance. The solution was very simple: stop doing the math!

Not controlling your finances strangely ends up by giving you a temporary sense that all is good. It feels just like my 1-year-old daughter who closes her eyes every time she wants to hide. As if the entire world only existed while she kept her eyes opened.

She believes that as soon as she closes her eyes, everything around her in the world suddenly disappears. It sounds stupid, right? Yet, a lot of people play that exact same kind of game when dealing with their finances. When the outcome of their budget isn't good, they pretend it doesn't even exist and they give up on controlling their finances. As if all the problems went away just because you're not looking at it.

I say it because I've been there. I know how it feels. But truth may come late, but never fails to show up.

Anyway, suddenly, when the situation became unsustainable, I decided that my story had to change. I felt I had no way out; I couldn't postpone it anymore. I moved to another apartment, I changed jobs, and things gradually came together - not without some setbacks, that is important to say.

I wrote my first financial control sheet in Excel and that changed my life. The first version was pretty basic: a column for the Budget and another one for the Actuals. There were mainly 3 different blocks of accounts: income, monthly expenses and investments.

Soon I came across a difficulty: what to do with non-recurring expenses? Just like that budget of the notebook I had made a few years earlier, I was not considering expenses like buying clothes, medicine or vacation trips, for example.

I also wanted to study, enroll in courses, buy books, etc. I needed to continue my professional career upwards and this would require greater investment in education, but I couldn't put any of these on the spreadsheet because I didn't know exactly in which month, I would spend that money. I had no idea of when I would buy new clothes, for instance.

So, I thought of an obvious solution: I would save a monthly amount to be used sporadically for these purposes. I called these new accounts "Savings for Short Term Expenses". I would treat this money as already spent and control it in a separate sheet.

As time is money, I used to keep this saved amount in a short-term investment and these savings would even generate some interest. And it would be easy for me to know how much I could spend on what. If on my spreadsheet, my balance in "savings for travel" was $400, that's what I had to spend, period.

This made it easier for me to make decisions. I would limit my expenses to what I had. No credit card loans, no payment in installments counting on money that I hadn't earned.

If my friends invited me to an international trip, I knew that with 400 dollars I couldn't go. But a domestic one, maybe I could.

Besides the income part, my financial spreadsheet now had 4 large groups:

(1) Income;

(2) Recurring Expenses;

(3) Savings for the short and mid-term expenses; and

(4) Long-term investments.

So, I organized my accounts in a sustainable way, balancing the present, the near future and the long run.

There was little left for each account, I have to say, but at least I had a clear idea of my financial situation. Unlike many people that when receive extra money start feeling the richest person on the planet, I had in mind what my future liabilities would be.

I wouldn't wait until I had earned more to start thinking of what I should do with this extra amount of money. I was already prepared to earn more. I knew exactly where any extra income or a sudden increase in my regular income would go to.

I created rules that made that money allocation automatic. As a result, I could also spend my money totally guilt free because I knew I wouldn't be taking it from any other goal.

This is what the budget is for, it gives us a clear idea of what has to be done in order to achieve the goals we want. And of course, it is extremely important to have control of your finances. A real, tangible control, something you can see whenever you want.

We value things a lot more when we can see them. The source of consumerism is that. Seeing real objects that you can touch and bring home immediately give us some satisfaction. It is a strong temptation. Even instant photos have turned trips, dinners, beach holidays and sports into "goods". There is now a much greater tendency to consume experience rather than products. Anyone with a cell phone can record any experience at any time.

Experiences today are more tangible and concrete than they were in the past and, therefore, we value them more. We keep talking about "millennials this" and " millennials that", but the truth is that no matter what your age is, you tend to value experience more than you used to in the past and social media plays a big part in this story. Some people use this artifice to show off, that is true. Something that in the past was only possible to do with material goods such as nice cars, houses and clothes from nice brands, today is often done through shared experiences on social networks.

And tangibility is so important that many companies keep targets printed and posted always in sight. A great strategy by the way. It consists of spreading throughout the company tables with the monitoring of the company's objectives and KPI's. Looking at an indicator every time makes us want to achieve it more efficiently. You will hardly forget its existence and since you will have to constantly look at it, it is better that the indicator is in the green.

Personal finances work the same way. Financial control transforms saving and investing into something concrete rather than an abstraction. Keeping track of your balance will bring you satisfaction. You will literally watch your financial life evolve!

It is very difficult to give up an immediate consumption or a certain standard of living when the counterpart of that is not so clear to you. Once there is a palpable and positive consequence as a result of a sacrifice, it becomes worthwhile and you will be motivated to achieve it!

Controlling is key because it makes your financial situation tangible. There are several ways to do it such as, in a notebook, apps on your cell phone, etc. My favorite is through Excel spreadsheets. I will share my recommendation later in the book and I will also explain my reasons for this preference. Now let's briefly talk about each big line you must control in your Financial Planning.

CHAPTER FIFTEEN

Your income

For salaried employees, budgeting income is often the easiest part of the planning. Unless a relevant part of the remuneration comes in the form of bonus and commissions, the value tends to be quite predictable.

The most important thing in this case is to know your net salary, already discounted from all taxes, including income taxes. On the internet there are several websites that provide net salary calculators. It's not your gross salary that matters at the end of the day. Here, some interesting and not always obvious tips:

- Do not budget overtime if the level of certainty is not really high. It's not worth to engage to something so variable and subjective, even if you do it with some recurrence. Unless it is written in the contract, nothing prevents your boss or the HR from changing their minds and deciding to end or reduce those overtime hours, ending up with this extra revenue from their employees.
- Non-cash benefits such as *meal tickets, transport, retirement plans and health insurance* should be measured and accounted for as income. In this way, it will become clearer how much you actually earn from your job. Many benefits are relevant and should influence your decision whether or not to change jobs, for example. After all, even if the salary elsewhere is greater, if you have to pay for health insurance and your meals, in the end it may not be worth changing, right?

It is necessary to have a breakdown as realistic as possible. The benefit will go into the account as income and expense at the same amount, which will not change your bottom line, but will give you a better idea of both the cost of your standard of living and the actual benefits that come from your job.

Likewise, if you have a loan or any other personal expense that is discounted directly from your paycheck, you must return this amount to your net salary and account for this loan as an expense.

That is, if your net salary should be $5,000, but at the end of the month you only receive $4,500 due to the payment of the monthly installment of $500 of a loan, the $500 will enter as expense and the $5,000 as salary.

A lot of people forget this and end up accounting only the $4,500 as revenue. But it is not that you are now with a lower salary, the problem is the debt you have. In that case, it has to be clear that the problem is not your income, but your level of expenses.

For Private Pension Plans the treatment should be very similar, the only difference is that instead of accounting it as an expense, it should be booked as Investment in Retirement Fund.

The fact that an amount is directly discounted from your salary does not mean that you are receiving less. It is very important to keep this in mind.

All this is to give you an idea of where you are.

Another thing that is important to say is that for some jobs, besides the salary you earn, it also yields intrinsic value in form of "experience". An experience that can be transformed into more income in the future via higher salaries and larger bonuses.

A lot of people do not see it this way, but experience is like compound interest. Generally, experienced professionals are worth more in the market. It varies a lot though. Some jobs will pay you roughly the same thing throughout your life, regardless of how experienced you are. Others don't. So, you should evaluate how much your current job is bringing knowledge for you and value to your CV.

There are experiences worth far more than others. On some occasions, especially early in a career, it could even be worth working for free for a while given all the learning and the number of opportunities that a good experience can provide for you.

By not realizing this, many people choose to follow shortcuts where they get paid better in the short term, but in jobs in which experience cannot be transformed into a future asset.

A good idea is to check how much the most experienced professionals in your area earn. Do this for homework. A good experience can be seen as extra profit. It's an invisible income. And if the return on the experience where you are doesn't please you, changing your path can be a way out.

I am not saying that "experience" should be accounted for in your Financial Spreadsheet. It is not that. The goal here is just to make you think about it. There is much more to consider beyond just your salary at the end of the month. Especially for those who have a vision of their future.

For all those whose source of income is any other type than salary, budgeting and controlling revenue become more complex and, at the same time, much more important.

When income is variable, it is essential to develop an expectation about how much you will receive in the coming months. Accurately accounting your actuals will be fundamental to give you good inputs to plan the future. Entrepreneurs, commissioned and liberal workers, etc. For all of these, this control is critical. Depending on how much you expect to receive, your future expenses will have to be adjusted and that's not an easy task.

Don't come with the excuse that it is impossible to guess how much you will earn. Don't even try! It is not guesswork, there must be prospects of gain, otherwise you wouldn't be there doing what you do, right?

I know some people think that being conservative is always good. Well, some level of conservatism is important when it comes to budgeting both revenues and expenses, but if the amount is high, it starts to play against you. You will always think about that buffer and this can ruin it all, causing your budget to fall into disrepair. Ideally, your budget should be as close to reality and expectation as possible.

A strict budget can be challenging and motivate you to chase after, and only in real cases of extreme doubt, be conservative.

Prepare for Income Tax

For all those who do not pay income taxes in full directly from the paycheck, and once a year usually have to pay an additional amount to the tax authorities, it is extremely important to prepare for this.

Project and deduct this amount from your net income and invest it throughout the year in order to avoid being "surprised" the following year by something that happens every year and more than that, something that could be easily assessed and prepared for.

Only income generates income taxes. If you have to pay it, it is a good sign, a sign that you have generated money! Think about it this way and only this way.

Some people strive to make good things look bad. Paying Income Tax is not the problem, the real problem is not generating income. Now look at the glass as half full and prepare for your obligations.

I'll repeat it as much as needed: <u>You can't be surprised by these things when you already know they exist</u>, whether you like to pay taxes or not.

Can moving to a higher tax bracket - due to an increase in my Gross Salary - cause me to end up with a lower net income?

Some people think that when their income increases by just enough to push them into a higher tax bracket, their overall take-home pay, will decrease.

No, no and no!

The great majority of countries in the world applies what is called a progressive tax rate system. In the US, it isn't different. In this type of system, an increase in income pushes you into a higher tax bracket, but you only pay the higher tax rate on that portion of your income that exceeds the income threshold for the next-highest tax bracket.

Here below, just as an example, you'll see the different Income Tax brackets for the US in 2019.

Individual Taxpayers

If Taxable Income Is Between:	The Tax Due Is:
0 - $9,700	10% of taxable income
$9,701 - $39,475	$970 + 12% of the amount over $9,700
$39,476 - $84,200	$4,543 + 22% of the amount over $39,475
$84,201 - $160,725	$14,382.50 + 24% of the amount over $84,200
$160,726 - $204,100	$32,748.50 + 32% of the amount over $160,725
$204,101 - $510,300	$46,628.50 + 35% of the amount over $204,100
$510,301 +	$153,798.50 + 37% of the amount over $510,300

The higher percentage is only applicable to the additional income and not the entire amount you earn. It is mathematically impossible to earn less with a higher gross income. Getting paid more might push you into a higher tax bracket but will certainly not lead you to a lower take-home pay.

CHAPTER SIXTEEN

Recurring Expenses

It's easy to recognize them, isn't it? They are very straight forward: recurring expenses are those that occur every month.

Wow!

Are they necessarily fixed expenses? Usually yes, but not always. Is your electricity bill a fixed cost? Yes and no. On one hand, you know you will incur this cost every month, so it is fixed in that sense, but its value varies according to the consumption, making it variable.

Your rent for example tends to be seen as a fixed cost. This is not wrong, but only valid for the short term. In the long term, it becomes variable since it is your decision to remain in the same place. You can always decide to move out or buy your own place. Even if you decide to stay in the same place it is likely that the rent amount will change according to inflation or any other index.

Dividing costs into fixed and variable can be interesting for analytical purposes, but not as clear and relevant as to break them down by periodicity. Because once you have prepared a Budget, almost every expense must become closer to be considered as fixed.

To create sustainable planning, the best way is to split your budget by recurrence. Sustainability in personal finance is a time balance. It is to maintain a good level of quality of life in the present without harming your future quality of life.

It is not just about having or not having debt. Spending everything you earn is not a proper financial life either. You must prepare at least for the expenses that do not happen every month, invest for your retirement and form a Safety Reserve.

A good budget is the one that finds this balance.

Therefore, the breakdown between present, near future and long term is translated by Recurring Expenses, Savings for Short and Medium Terms Expenses and Long-Term Investments.

Recurring Expenses are a kind of a proxy for your standard of living. Therefore, the ideal is to maintain a more or less static level. Ideally, it will be a fixed amount, a value you should know by heart.

A lot of people think that earning more is the only possible solution to their financial problems. Not everyone realizes that a dollar saved has the same impact as an additional dollar of income. So, before blaming your low salary for financial problems, make sure you have stretched your expenses in the search of the best cost-benefit deals.

Now, I'm going to walk you through each of the most common recurring expenses.

Rent

This is usually one of the highest costs and therefore it is extremely important to monitor it.

If your situation is unsustainable and you have nowhere else to cut, it is likely that the rent you are paying is not in line with your financial situation.

A value that exceeds 30% of the Net Income of the family is a very bad sign. In cities like San Francisco, London, NYC or Paris, you might have to pay a little more than that, but not much more!

Now, I don't recommend it to be your first move because it is costly financially and emotionally. Moving is never easy, but sometimes it is your only chance of creating a sustainable financial future. In addition, a new home can be a symbol of a new beginning, a new life. Face it as temporary, just until you get your financial life organized.

Groceries

Surely you have been to the supermarket to buy one thing and left it with a lot of other things you had no idea you needed. Without planning, people often get lost in the supermarket overspending on things they don't need.

The best way to avoid waste is to create a shopping list with things you really need. It's an old recipe, but believe me, it still works. Don't put on the list of what you want, but instead, start with what you can spend. Set the amount beforehand and then, create a list that fits that amount. Stick to the list, temporarily avoid unnecessary items and try to change expensive products for cheaper ones.

If the list does not help you from buying other stuff, another strategy would be to pay your market expenses in cash. Withdraw beforehand the maximum amount you intend to spend and leave your credit cards at home. You will be amazed at how selective you can be when there really is no other option. With limited cash in your wallet you will leave everything on the shelf that is not essential.

The supermarket has a certain kind of magic for some who are usually great at sticking to their budget everywhere else, but once they get into the supermarket, they feel free to take whatever they want as if there was no limit.

In the end, when they realize how expensive it was, they blame inflation, taxes, the Government, even if they bought far beyond what was necessary. Keep that in mind: $10 spent in the supermarket impacts your budget in the same way as $10 spent anywhere else.

For most of us, I think this is a behavior that comes from when we were kids and teenagers and we used to look at "home food" as free food. But as the saying goes, there is no free lunch (in this case, literally). There has never been and never will be, so you better realize that.

There is nothing wrong with having some luxury when you can afford it. And plus, if you choose that spending on food is your priority, who am I to contest? But make sure you realize it is your choice and that there is a trade-off with the other accounts.

If it's not among your main objectives, control it. Sometimes the adjustment is needed only for the short term, until the financial situation is restored.

It could be a big issue. Groceries are one of the hardest costs to admit that there is a problem. There is the "but that is the only one I like", "I don't spend money with anything else", "this brand is a lot better" and so on. Other excuses often come hidden in thoughts like, "sometimes the cheaper is more expensive." This is true for some cases, but I my impression is that people think this way more often than they should. Most of the time, it is only to justify a more costly choice. Usually it is the result of good marketing. I always say that sometimes cheaper is more expensive, but the truth is that the expensive is always expensive.

Cell phone

Over the years, most products and services have become increasingly expensive due to inflation readjustments. Mobile service has been an exception.

Switching offers is often a good deal and simple to do. Usually it's the first step for those who decide to put their financial life in order. Just go to the big Companies websites and compare cost x benefit. And… action!

Fixed Telephone, Cable TV and internet

Let's face it, do you still really need a Fixed telephone?

For most people, I don't think so. If it is possible to cancel yours, this will be an easy saving.

If you still need it for any reason, it's worth researching the possibility of prepaid fixed plans for those who don't use much.

Regarding cable TV, reflect on if you really need your current package of channels or if you could move to a cheaper one.

Streaming has emerged in the last few years as an excellent replacement for some more advanced Cable TV packages. It is worth researching there as well. Surprisingly, believe it or not, Cable-Fixed-Internet bundles are not always cheaper. It's possible to save money when combining stand-alone offers. Start checking what fits you better. The market is very dynamic.

Pocket money

Some financial planners suggest that you write down all your expenses, no matter how small they are.

Latte is their preferred enemy!

I personally think this is way too much. In the beginning, for people who have over consuming problems, it can be a good recommendation, but once your financial life is under control, there is no need to continue with this.

A good Financial Plan simplifies your life. I say: give yourself a weekly allowance. It will turn into fixed expenses, what many planners call Variable Expenses, which, by the way, they always tell you to cut.

You don't have to necessarily cut the beer and the barbecue with friends or dinner with your boy or girlfriend on the weekends. Just create a limit that is consistent with your Budget for it.

You should not worry too much about where that money went to. It is the only part of the budget for you to freely spend without having to worry. Respect it with the same discipline you'll use for your savings! Don't spend more than your allowance, but never use it to save or invest either. Investment is to invest and your pocket money is to be spent. If there is money left over at the end of the week, great, you will be able to spend more in the following one! That's the spirit!

Never use your pocket money to invest!

It is to be used with small expenses and with leisure like dinner, cinema, theater, night clubs, etc. Exactly like the pocket money you might have received from your parents when you were a teenager.

The value will vary from person to person, from income to income. The most important thing is to have the discipline of not overspending.

To make it easier, every Monday, I go to the bank and I withdraw my allowance, I put it in my wallet and in this way, I have full over it. When it's gone, it's gone. That's it and "sorry guys, I'm not meeting you in the pub tonight because I have no money left."

Why lie? Tell them the truth, and if they insist, recommend this book to them!

Donations

Look for a cause you truly believe in to make monthly donations.

This will do you good and you will feel that the responsibility that you carry in taking good care of your finances is also with those who need it the most. I like to get involved in projects that encourage people to become independent, prioritizing teaching how to fish instead of just giving the fish. I like to help medical aid as well.

Besides, whoever donates money is happier. This was the result of a Harvard Business School study in 136 countries. Warren Buffet, Bill Gates and many other billionaires and millionaires have the habit of donating money.

Remember the guys in the arena. Some point the finger to show how those who do, could have done any better. Others go there and actually do it!

If not money, try to find some room to donate a little of your time. Include helping others as a responsibility for you and you'll see how magical things will happen to your life. And, most importantly, how small acts can be impactful in other people's lives.

Credit Card

Creating an account called "credit card" is a very bad start. Credit card is not an expense but a means of payment such as cash, check or debit cards. You don't spend money on the credit card, but through it.

The clothes you bought and shouldn't is the problem, be it via cash or credit card. This confusion often makes the credit card a villain when in fact it is innocent.

So, if you're going to create a credit card account on your spreadsheet, just put the card's annuity there, not the total amount of your bill.

The credit card is an enemy of people with no control, but, in fact, it can be a great ally for those who plan well.

Some benefits of using a credit card:

- **I get time to pay**. Credit Cards are free short-term loan. And time is money, right? Do you have an idea of what it means? That means that if I put my money into investments that yields daily interest, I can get money through using my credit card instead of using the cash I have invested. Interests are not huge, I know, but if you turn using your credit card into a habit, over time you will have saved a good amount of money just by exchanging the debit card for the credit card. Money has value in time and paying tomorrow <u>without interest</u> is better than paying today.
- **Easy to track**. By concentrating my purchases on credit cards, I don't have to look at my account's balance every day. You don't have to remind yourself where your cash went to either. Once a month, I take my credit card bill and enter it on a spreadsheet categorizing how much was spent and on what.
- **I receive points and rewards.** From time to time, I change my points for miles, and I travel for free. Options are unlimited, some cards offer you cash back – which by the way, tends to be the best option – or discount on hotels, car rentals, purchases, you name it. You can also have access to free travel insurance and warranties. All that just because you chose to use a credit card while leaving your cash invested.

These reasons make credit cards my favorite method of payment. I use it for everything, except for my pocket money. However, it can be your best friend or your worst enemy.

It depends on <u>how you use it</u>!

As long as you manage them well, they'll be one of the best tools you'll have. But if you don't completely pay off your bill at the end of the month, you'll be screwed, charged with one of the highest interest rates of the economy. Even worse, some companies will also tack on whopping fee every time you miss a payment, and that fee can get as high as $30.

For the people that don't have full control of their finances, it's also very easy to overuse their credit cards and end up in big debt.

Honestly, sooner or later you'll have to admit that it has never been the credit card's fault. It has always been yours. You have been misusing it. A lot of people around the globe do the same. That's why I always recommend the following rules:

- **Don't use your credit card to spend money you don't have yet**. Limit its use to the example I gave before, that is when you have the money, but you prefer to leave it invested and use your credit card as the free short-term loan tool it can be.
- **If they offer you a discount for using cash, pay in cash**! Discounts for paying in cash are the same as interest in paying with credit cards in disguise. It's a marketing ploy, that's all.
- **Never, <u>I said, never</u> miss a payment and never pay only the minimum**. Pay off the total amount of your credit card on time and you should be fine. The best thing you could do is to set up automatic payments for all your credit cards.

Use your credit cards wisely. The ones with no annual fees and with more rewards are the best choices. Also, I think that having 2 credit cards is a good number. Having too many can make you lose control.

Other expenses

Other typical recurring expenses are utilities, transportation costs like fuel or public transport, taxi, and Uber, or, most likely, a combination of all of these.

If you need to cut your hair or go to the barber every month, it is also worth creating an account for this purpose. If you go to the gym or do some other sport, bank fees, courses or any other expenses that occur every month. Find room for each of them!

From the moment you begin to account for your expenses, you will probably have some questions as to where to enter some of them.

For example, if you use an Uber on a trip and you have a budget for Travel and another for Uber, how do you account for that: as a travel expense or as a regular transportation expense? It all depends on what you have envisioned when you created your Budget. There is a certain subjectivity in this.

As I see it, in this specific example, the main question you have to ask yourself is: did this Uber expense only occurred because you were traveling, or would you have incurred this expense otherwise? Eating a hot dog in Rome can be interpreted in the same way as eating one in your neighborhood: you should use your pocket money.

Well, by the way, don't eat hot dogs in Rome, go for Lasagnas!

To summarize this chapter, recurring expenses are fixed, semi-fixed or variable expenses that occur every month. They are relatively easier to remember when you are planning.

Some other expenses do not happen every month and many people end up forgetting to prepare for them.

Therefore, it is very important to talk about it so that you never forget to reserve a part of your monthly income for them.

CHAPTER SEVENTEEN

Savings for Short & Medium Term Expenses

Some costs occur on an annual basis or at least in another frequency other than every month, and very often people forget to prepare for that. Everything that differs from the regular monthly expenses, ends up complicating your financial planning.

Most people are typical bill payers. All they want is to receive a bill to be paid at the end of the month. It's the only way they know how to organize their finances.

The fact that some expenses do not occur on a monthly basis does not prevent you from preparing for them every month. All you have to do is budget an annual amount you intend or will have to pay and divide it by the number of months of the year. This will give you a closer look at what your costs really are.

Here are some of the most common non-recurring expenses by which you must separate a monthly amount for:

Car maintenance

The decision to have a car requires some analysis that goes beyond having the money to buy it. You need to be able to maintain it without it becoming an anchor in your financial planning that prevents you from evolving.

In addition to the insurance, having a car means from time to time spending money with oil change, additive, balancing and changing tires, among others. These expenses cannot surprise you. Everyone who owns a car should be aware of their existence and prepare for them.

Each car has a different type of maintenance cost depending on the brand, age, etc. Think about these costs and their periodicity. Then, break them into an equivalent amount per month.

So, if you estimate that you will need new tires every 4 years and they cost $240, save $5 per month for this.

In addition to these expenses, you can also foresee some expenses with repairing the vehicle from small crashes. So, even if something undesirable happens to the car, you'll already be prepared to fix it.

Owning a car is knowing that sometimes it breaks down. Chances are high that at some point even if it is not very frequent, at least something is going to break, and you will have to buy some spare parts you didn't even know existed.

The best response to this is to prepare to face all these costs. Owning a car means a lot more than just having the money to buy it. You have to be prepared to maintain it and it is not cheap.

Property Maintenance

Just like the car, your house also needs maintenance. Whether it is a visit from the plumber, the replacement of furniture or of broken dishes.

Then, there is property tax.

You have to be aware and ready to face all of them.

Travel

At the beginning of every year I formulate the trips I want to take on my holidays and research how much they would cost me.

After adjusting the destination not only to what I want but also to what I can afford without hurting my other goals, I then divide the total cost by 12 and start saving every month.

In general, I begin with a simpler travel budget, but if later I happen to have more money, I end up upgrading my trips.

Also, when plans are to travel abroad, a good idea is to immediately start buying the currency of the destination every month to dilute the risk of sudden variations on the exchange rate harming your travel expenses.

Something worth thinking about is that for longer trips (of at least 2 weeks) you kind of end up saving some Recurring Expenses. Despite the travel expenses you are going to have, you save electricity at home, your weekly pocket money, transportation, etc. It is worth considering this savings when you make your travel budget. It is important to quantify to get a good idea about this value. There are people who know that this saving exists but end up thinking that it is much higher than it actually is.

Education

Every type of investment should have some place in your budget, but if I had to pick one as the most important, I would definitely pick this one.

Simply put this in your head: You are your main asset. You are the source of all money you will make, the source of every joy and every love you will have.

Invest in yourself!

You don't speak a foreign language? Prepare to learn one.

Don't have a college degree? Get ready to get it.

There are great options for distance learning nowadays. Another good idea might be to prepare to study abroad. There are many great universities in Europe with prices more affordable than in the US. There are also several courses offered in English in countries like Germany, Spain, Netherlands or France, and you can at the same time: study for less, open your mind to a totally different culture and learn a foreign language while you enjoy a fun and enriching experience!

Too late for you? Consider that option for your kids if you have them.

Most important, however, is that although some degrees may be fundamental, we are already getting to a point where degrees are serving us less and less, which is not a bad thing.

What really matters in the end is your knowledge and it is available today in thousands of different ways.

Invest in yourself! Invest in yourself! Invest in yourself!

Most people don't really need that many certificates or diplomas. Kindle, for example, will give you access to many titles from all around the globe right in the palm of your hand. I'm always reading on the bus, in the bank, wherever I have to wait.

A lot of people spend time on social networks. They are important in small doses but very time consuming if used with no control.

So, here is a good tip: change a good portion of the time you spend with social media for digital reading.

I totally agree with what I heard Seth Godin saying the other day: If people only realize how much buying a book is a bargain!

For $15, $20 you have access to a content that can change you and your life forever!

And everyone who decided to commit to the long process of writing a book is because they have something interesting to share. Believe me. Every time you finish reading one book, you become a new person.

Also, there are good apps such as Coursera that gives you access to courses from the best universities in the world at very affordable prices.

Investing in education is mandatory. It is part of building a better future. And if you think education is expensive, try ignorance.

Gifts and Parties

Another non-recurring expense is with presents and parties. Wedding anniversaries, the children's birthdays, Christmas gifts, Mother's and Father's Day, friends' weddings, etc.

Anyway, all these dates mean expenses with gifts or celebrations. Prepare for them.

Health

If you have ever had a situation of making adjustments in your personal finance and ended up getting sick in the middle of the way, having to spend a lot of money on medicines, then you know the importance of this account.

Unfortunately, it is often likely we may get at least the flu or a cold. It is good to have some money saved to cover this kind of expense if needed.

Just remember, the monthly payment for health insurance is a recurring expense. Your savings for Health are meant to be used in every other expense you'll have that is not covered by your insurance.

Clothing

Another expense we have from time to time is with clothing. As the days go by, your clothes become old and you will have to replace them for new ones.

Don't forget that: being well dressed changes the way people look at you whether you agree with it or not.

Accessories and Equipment

The same happens with electronic equipment like cell phones, computers, etc. From time to time, they will break or become obsolete and will have to be replaced.

In addition, new possibilities arise with new technologies.

Focus on the type of equipment that will help you increase your productivity at home by reducing the time spent with home duties. Some examples of things that I have at home that save me some precious time: Garment Steamer for clothes; Instant Pressure Cookers; Dish and clothes washing machines; etc.

This could be what I call smart spending.

Mid-term expenses

Most of these mid-term expenses are one-off experiences such as a wedding party or a round-the-world trip.

Regarding the wedding party, my suggestion is to plan it very carefully. It is a great day for everyone, and we want it to be perfect in all means. But the most important aspect in all this is your significant other. Don't forget that. The wedding is usually just the beginning of a life-long partnership. Keep that in mind.

For me and Alice, we wanted to get married in a up close and personal ceremony. So, we did it, just the two of us, in a desert beach in an Island called Ilha Grande, 2 hours from Rio de Janeiro, in Brazil. We had the trees, the mountains and the sea in a beautiful sunny evening in August. It meant a lot for us. It is the most remarkable memory of our lives together. We have always been used to being surrounded with friends and family all the time. But that was our moment. We didn't have to spend a lot of money for that either, but that was not the main reason. We did it the way we wanted it to be. But some people feel the need of spending mountains of money in a day. No problem if that is your dream. That is what we live for: accomplishing our goals! But my advice is: watch out. When we start a life together there is just so many things in the horizon. We'll move together, we'll feel the need for more space, children might show up sooner or later. If you're not prepared for all that, money can be a real problem, and this can turn out to be a reason for divorce, something we already discussed about. Your marriage should be more valuable than your wedding. Start your couple life in a healthy situation. You can always through a wedding party to share your joy with your friends and family in the future in the 10- or 15-years anniversary when you'll probably feel you're more financially stabilized.

A funny thing is that people just love subscriptions. They're willing to pay a high amount of money in exchange of unlimited consumption. For them, paying it gives the idea of receiving stuff for free. This is very weird, I know. Some of my friends, simply love to go to these all-you-can eat steakhouses, where you pay a high amount of money to eat whatever you can. And they do eat a lot, even beyond what brings satisfaction for them. So, once I suggested we went to a regular restaurant and used that money to order whatever we wanted. But they declined. "What is the point of spending the same amount of money in a place where service is limited?" The thing is that in a all-you-can eat, there is no limit, I know, but we human beings have always our limit! In the end, it doesn't matter! Most of the times, you accept to pay more just to have the feeling of freedom. When you are in a à-la-carte restaurant, you won't be willing to order that much because once you are satisfied, why would you pay to order more food? What people don't realize is that's exactly what they do in an all-you-can-eat.

We all tend to do that. I have a Netflix account at home. As I write this book, Netflix charges $12.99 a month, in the Standard package. I and Alice usually watch it once in the weekends only accounting for something close to $ 3 per session at best because sometimes, we travel in the weekend or we just decide to do other stuff. Still is worth. But another day, I wanted to watch something paid in Youtube instead. They wanted to charge me $2.50 to watch it and my reaction was "no way I'll pay it!!". So, I am OK with the commitment to pay a higher price every month to have unlimited service, but I refuse to pay a lower price for a pay-per-use. The thing is that there is no such thing as unlimited, this is something purely psychological. Ultimately, our time is limited to 24 hours a day, and we still have to take some rest and sleep anyway. But using the word "unlimited" is a better marketing pitch than saying you can use it up to 16 hours a day.

But Netflix doesn't really hurt, after all $12.99 for Netflix or $7.50 for a pay-per-use, I am actually spending $5.49 just to get the word "unlimited" in my life. Same thing for all-you-can-eat restaurants, if doesn't happen every week, so OK. It's a limited effect. But when it comes to higher expenses such as having a car, this could hurt.

I know people that go to work using public transport and still keep a car parked in their garage. The fixed cost related to having a car can be something close to $400 a month, just with maintenance, insurance and depreciation (the amount of money in which the car value decreases through time). And then, there is fuel and parking expenses, and that amount can quickly jump to at least $700 if you use it only on the weekends. What if you decided to use Uber instead? Do you know what would happen? You would refuse to spend more than $100 every weekend to use Uber, that's what would happen. You would think twice about moving around every time you need to. Even if you would be saving money if compared to having a car.

I'm not saying that everybody should sell their cars and exchange it for Uber. Some people use their cars to work and travel constantly. In some places, there is not even Uber service. And I also know that deep inside, a car is still a symbol of status and some people prefer to show others how they are doing well, even when they are actually not doing good at all.

But my point is that when costs become transparent, we become reluctant to spend. When they are hidden in a bill disguised as "unlimited", we see them as unavoidable costs that we simply have to incur for living. It's weird, but we prefer to give up a higher amount of money in exchange for having less flexibility in our budget. Shouldn't it be the other way around? This is so not right. The more pay-per-use, the clearer will that cost be to you. And then, just move to subscriptions if you are spending more than its fee.

Others

It doesn't stop here. You have to save for all expenses that you will have in the short and medium term. Any short- or medium-term goals or commitments that you may have should become a reason for saving!

CHAPTER EIGHTEEN

Survival first

A businessman was standing at the pier of a small coastal village when a little boat with one fisherman docked. Inside the boat were several large yellow fin tunas.

The fisherman, tired from his work took a seat close to the businessman.

"How long did it take you to catch all this fish?" The businessman asked.

"I was lucky today; it took me just a few hours"

"Why don't you stay out longer and catch more fish, then?" again asked the businessman.

"Why should I if I have enough to support my family's immediate needs?" The fisherman replied.

"If you spend more time fishing every day, with the additional proceeds you could buy a bigger boat and get even more fishes. Then, you could buy several boats, and eventually you would have a fleet of fishing boats."

"Instead of selling your catch to a middleman you would sell directly to the consumers, eventually opening your own can factory. You would control the product, processing and distribution. Your company would grow until a certain stage where you could sell it for a high price to somebody else."

"But what then, what would I do after selling the Company?"

"Then - answered the businessman - you would retire, move to a small coastal fishing village and fish for a few hours every day."

This is a well-known story that shows us a lot of things, starting from the value of the simple things in life. So, people usually buy the point of view of the simple fisherman, after all, why is the point of doing all that to finish where already is?

But the businessman is not stupid. We, human beings, tend to think that other people's lives are always easier than ours. When we think about the life of a fisherman living in a small village, what comes naturally to our minds is tranquility, peace of mind and an easy and restful life. No traffic jam, no violence, no rush...

We rarely think of all the adversities of someone who also has problems like any of us. Does he always fish enough to properly feed his family? Even if he does, is he sure that he'll be able to do so in the following morning? Is it likely to stress him? You bet it does!

The point that I want to make here is: One activity can be relaxing or stressing depending on the way we look at them. Things in life have no meaning except the meaning we give them.

Objective number 1 for every human being in life is survival. It doesn't matter who you are and whether you are conscious of it or not. And not only humans, but all living species. On the other hand, stress is the way our body responds to danger, a reaction for survival. Uncertainties, fears, feeling of weakness and even Tim Urban's Panic Monster are the root causes of stress! Of course that the less level of stress there is in our lives, the better. But how to do that?

For the fisherman, the truth is that he doesn't fish for fun but for survival. It is a huge difference! It is his work and it's as stressful as any other one.

From that he earns his living which is never guaranteed until the moment he gets home with the fish that will feed his family. The next day, he'll repeat the same ritual. What will happen to this guy when one day fishes don't appear for him? What if he has a disease for several days when he is not able to work? What if his boat breaks? What will happen to him and his family when he becomes old?

All of these questions are the ones we ask ourselves in our urban lives, but we like to think that a fisherman doesn't have these issues, right? But he does.

The suggestion of the businessman is to release from the fishing activity the element of the need for survival. When you're rich and decide to retire, your needs are met. Moving to a small village is then an option and fishing will no longer be work, but leisure. The advice of the businessman now doesn't look as stupid as it could have sounded in the beginning.

Some people say the secret for success is to do what you love. But they forget to say that it is a lot easier to love what you do when you are successful.

Good results stimulate us, we all love doing stuff that we feel we are good at. But besides that, once you have reached a certain level of success, the results of your work are not anymore linked to your survival needs. When you have reached financial success, survival is guaranteed, and the meaning of your work is another one. You have gone to another level.

When the focus of your work is not your own survival, you become free to realize how meaningful it can be.

We are all born with nothing built by ourselves. In our early ages, survival can only be provided from somebody else. Once we grow up, we are expected to find our independence and if that is not the case, it will be a source of frustration. Dependence in adult life leads to stress.

Our number one goal in life is to guarantee our own survival. This is the main source of stress in our lives. The best way to escape it is having an organized financial life. People with a higher level of financial independence can choose where to work. They can do what they want, but this is only possible because they've done their homework first which is "do what you need" to then reach a certain level where you can choose what you want.

There are two types of behaviors that I have no respect for, and I can easily foresee what will happen in the lives of people who fall for this kind of thinking. The first one is the spoiled young adult that leaves university convinced that he will only work with what he enjoys. This is usually a recipe for disaster. This young boy or girls will learn at some point that one of the most important things in life is to be independent. They will also realize that not everything that looks fun from outside is actually fun when you have to do it for a living, such as in the fisherman tale. As times passes, they will start seeing other people succeeding and in some point their self-esteem will diminish. If they take too long to identify what went wrong in the path they chose, they'll end up witnessing a curious case: Their friends that have chosen boring activities will move to do what they want to do, while themselves, having chosen to start life doing what they loved, obliged to change to professions they don't like at all in order to find their independence.

One thing I learned is that if you do what's easy first, your life will be hard but if you choose to do what's hard first, your life will then become easier.

The problem is that most people look at their careers as a definite thing. As if their professions will define forever who they are, but no one is doomed to do one single thing for their entire life.

Work delivering pizzas, bussing tables, dish washing and so on will not define you forever. Instead, they are very promising activities in the early ages. I've done them all. Afterwards, if you have the opportunity to go to a University, you can get a different kind of job, usually one that pays you better. Once you have become completely independent from anybody else's money, you start saving and investing. At some point, having enough saved and with more experience, you can start your own business and once it gives you the first signs of success you are able to resign from your job.

Work hard and, in the end, you'll end up able to do whatever you like to do.

It sounds like a reasonable plan, doesn't it?

That's how reality is and honestly it is so damn fair. No one comes into life just to do what they ~would like~ to do. Doing what you like is an achievement, not a right.

Survival first!

The second type of person I don't understand is the one that spends his entire life doing the same thing he doesn't even like over and over every day. He is the opposite of the former because he didn't choose to do what he wanted but instead he doesn't believe anymore that there is a way out of where he stands. The way he sees it is as if he has been condemned to do it for eternity due to some kind of sorcery. And what's worse, he tries to convince everyone around that this is just how life works.

Boring, boring, boring.

It's possible to see our professional lives as different cycles, think of it: We should all start with some physical student jobs, then migrate to a more technical and skillful profession to learn and help other people's Company, we then are more experienced and financially prepared to start our own business and once our business is at a certain level of maturity that it doesn't even need us anymore, we can do the activity we love – for fun and meaning!

It is a journey to achievement for whoever believes it.

Dare to do what you love but be realistic.

You know some people skip College and sometimes even resign from work they don't like with the excuse that "they are chasing their dreams". Well, it could be the best thing you'll ever do if your dream is somehow realistic. But test it first! And as response comes back positively, you take the next step. If first results are frustrating, hmm… it could be a bad sign.

Most people use the examples of Steve Jobs, Bill Gates, Mark Zuckerberg and so many others to justify why they are quitting their current activities. They fantasize that by quitting the day-to-day normal life, they'll become the next billionaires.

Easier said than done. All you need is a little research into the life of these guys and you'll realize that they have never quit anything to start thinking of what they wanted to do next.

The reason why they quit is because they were already having enough success in whatever they were working at in parallel. They didn't achieve success because they had left university and the traditional path. Instead, they decided to quit exactly because they had achieved some success first. If you're considering quitting, you better think before if you have really found your way.

If you have, no problem. Go for it, man.

My point is very simple: Find what you love and do whatever it takes to get there. Do not expect life to arrange things for you. Fight for it!

And don't stop doing whatever you are currently doing until you have a plan at the risk of finding yourself completely lost, lonely and with low self-esteem.

Remember, life is like riding a bicycle: to keep your balance you must keep moving.

This is true for all matters of your life from academic and professional choices to building your investment strategy.

No one should start investing looking for the long term, if they don't have their Safety Reserve guaranteed or if they do not have any saving for short term expenses. It is a sequence.

Survival first!

CHAPTER NINETEEN

Investments

Last but certainly not least, let's now talk about investments.

Many people, in fact, anxious to get rich, want to start by the end. One of the questions I hear the most is "what should I invest in"? Without any context, this question means absolutely nothing to me. There is no such thing as the best investment, but there are several different great investment choices depending on a list of different features.

The quality of your investments depends first and foremost on your current financial situation and your future objectives. No one can think of starting, for example, to invest in the stock market if they are still paying the minimum of the credit card bill. It's a contradiction.

At this point in the book, you must have understood this, already (hopefully).

The first question you should be able to answer is "where am I?".

The second is "where do I want to go?".

Financially speaking, the answer to the first question is in your Control. You have to have full control of how much your income and your recurring and non-recurring expenses are.

For the second question the answer is planning: Where do you want to be in the future?

Investment management is "how to get there". Investing alone will not make any sense without your personal financial control.

Before discussing all the investment needs and the best financial products for each of them, I think it's worth going back to George S. Clason's Babylon for a while.

According to history books, there has never been a richer and more glamorous city than ancient Babylon. A city, with no relevant natural resources, no large forest, no mines, not even stones to be used in construction, but that was located in the middle of a natural trade route. Its wealth came entirely from there. This is an excellent example of how willing men and women with clear goals, can use whatever resources to achieve what they want.

But not all of its population had access to this wealth. A few men held much more than others. And the question is what did these men know that set them apart from the others? Knowledge is undoubtedly the greatest source of wealth a man can have. Understanding this was the first step for the main character in Clason's book, Arkad, to become the richest man in Babylon.

In the story, his life changed thanks to his hunger for understanding where wealth came from and what the rich did to become rich. In a dialogue, still poor, Arkad asks a rich man for guidance. The man then tells him that the secret is to pay himself first. This was the most important and the simplest advice given to Arkad in a passage that has become one of the greatest classics in financial literature.

In full, because it's worth it, the rich man told him:

'I found the road to wealth when I decided that a part of all I earned was mine to keep.'

Arkad asked, 'But is this all?'

'This alone is enough to turn the heart of a sheep herder into the heart of a man who could even lend money.'

'But, after all, all that I gain is mine to keep. No? "Replied Arkad.

'Far from it,' said the rich man, 'do not you pay the Garment maker? And sandal-maker? Do not you pay for the things you eat? Can you live in Babylon without spending money? How much did you save in the last month? On the last year? Fool. You pay everyone but yourself. You work for others as well as a slave who works for his master to give him what to eat and wear. If you keep 10% of what you earn, how much would you have in 10 years?'

'Same as I get in a year?' Replied Arkad.

'You say only half truth. Every piece of gold you save will be a slave working for you. Every copper it earns is its child that also can earn for you. If you would become wealthy, then what you save must earn, and its children must earn, that all may help to give to you the abundance you crave. A part of all you earn is yours to keep. It should be not less than a tenth no matter how little you earn. It can be as much more as you can afford. Pay yourself first. Do not buy from the clothes maker and the sandal-maker more than you can pay out of the rest and still have enough for food and charity and penance to the gods. Wealth, like a tree, grows from a tiny seed. The first copper you save is the seed from which your tree of wealth shall grow. The sooner you plant that seed the sooner shall the tree grow. And the more faithfully you nourish and water that tree with consistent savings, the sooner may you bask in contentment beneath its shade.

Don't forget it: 'Wealth is like a tree. It grows from tiny seed. Feed it constantly with more savings and it will flourish.'"

(The Richest Man in Babylon, George Clason)

Very interesting, but now you might be thinking "what happens if there's nothing left to invest at the end of the month"?

Wait a minute... nothing left???

What do you mean by "nothing left"? Money is a limited resource for everyone, my friend. Some people decide what they will do with it and take the responsibility of directing it. Money is not left in a magical way. It is your responsibility to save it.

But monthly bills consume everything you earn? Commit to reducing them.

Is rent a value you cannot afford? Move somewhere else. Don't want to? Whose problem is it? Come on, I know it is not easy, but no one ever said it would be.

There is no such thing as "leftover" when talking about money. Only for those who prefer to take a passive attitude in life. "It's not my fault, prices are high" or "my salary is low" may even momentarily satisfy some hearts, but they do not solve the problem.

When planning, it will be up to you, the only one responsible for your financial life, to decide how much to invest, how much to save and what lifestyle you will have.

Our life is not a simple result of luck, it is the result of our efforts over time. It takes discipline, patience and dedication.

If you do not have money to invest, search for it. A man who earns $2 thousand per month will say that it is not possible to save. One that earns $4 thousand will say the same thing.

However, what does the man who earns $2 thousand to live with this amount that the one who earns $ 4 thousand is not able to do?

There are many who believe that it is not possible to live on less than what they earn, however each once of us receives a different amount of money.

It is always possible!! You just have to find a way.

Saving and investing are possible for those who are determined. And there are at least three good reasons to invest:

1) Create a Safety Reserve for any emergency, but mainly for momentarily losing your source of income.

2) Create your own Retirement Fund to maintain your standard of living when time comes that you are no longer able (or do not want) to create wealth anymore.

3) Increase your standard of living by creating additional sources of income other than your job. Complementary income generated by your investments.

Each one with its totally specific characteristic. The first two are focused on security. The third focused on the return.

Therefore, the answer to the question "Where should I invest" can only be "It depends".

In addition, I will speak of a fourth type of investment that is the investment in real estate. It could fit into other reasons as described above, but due to its particularity and popularity, I will talk about it separately.

Investing purpose #1: Safety Reserve

Let me put it this way: your salary is the return you receive for the time you spend producing for the company you work for. If one day they no longer need your service for whatever reason, they will dismiss you.

Yes, as simple as that, just the same way you would if you came across some opportunity that you found more interesting in terms of finance, career or quality of life.

If you are an entrepreneur, it is the same for your clients.

The rules of the game are clear and known beforehand by all players. You must be prepared for this game according to its rules.

So, if one day you get fired, it is no use to dramatize, feel desolate, wronged, a victim etc.

None of this.

Well, feeling bad for a while is natural, even justifiable, but for being unprepared, no excuses, Mister. You need a Safety Reserve for this possibility that is real. It is also nice to have a plan B.

If a resignation knocks on your door, what will you do with your life? Find another job, change your profession, take the opportunity to take a foreign language course abroad, finally take your project to open your company from paper?

Once your current life is organized, it is important to take the time to put together a protection for future moments of possible instabilities like these. We all know that life is made of ups and downs, it is up to us to prepare ourselves during the moments of calm for the most difficult times that can ever come. The right time to fix a broken roof is when the sun is still shining. When the rain comes, it will be too late.

For this reason, we all have to have a financial Safety Reserve for periods of turbulence. Something ranging from 3 to 12 months of your average cost of living.

Anyone who feels that they have a more or less steady income from a secure source; such as a retirees or government employee, should have the equivalent of 3 months of their monthly expenses.

Most of the private sector workers are recommended to have the equivalent to 6 months. It is considered to be a reasonable time to get back into the labor market in case something happens.

Entrepreneurs, self-employed and salesmen who earn a large part of their income through commissions and whose income tends to be more unstable, should consider forming savings equivalent to 9 to 12 months depending on how risky the source of income is.

How much time do I have to build this reserve?

Forming a safety reserve is the priority in the hierarchy of the investment world. It is obvious because an emergency could happen tomorrow to any of us. Besides that, if this reserve is never used - and that is what we all hope for - it can still be used for improving your standard of living in retirement.

The opposite is not so obvious though. It is far more difficult to use risky assets for safety purposes and sometimes, as we'll discuss later, it is not even possible due to the lack of liquidity.

So, I suggest that for those who need to build their safety reserve, use 100% of your investments only for this purpose until you can reach at least a third of the amount you need.

If the goal is to build the most common which is the 6-months reserve, commit yourself fully to it until you have the equivalent of at least 2 months.

Once you've met 1/3 of your total target, continue saving until you complete your safety reserve, but now you can do it in a slower pace. You no longer need to invest 100% of your investments in a Safety Reserve. You can, in parallel, start investing also for your retirement.

How long you will take to reach all the needed amount is a decision that is up to you. Go as fast as you really can and don't commit to doing something that you are not going to be able to do. Set a reasonable deadline for yourself. I suggest that nothing longer than one year to complete the first 1/3 and four years to complete everything.

Once you hit the set amount - and as long as your average expenses remain unchanged - you can stop saving for this purpose.

Don't forget that for every increase in your standard of living, you will need a proportional increase in your Safety Reserve in order to keep your financial life always balanced.

So, for a salaried person to increase her average monthly spend by $100, she should also increase her reserve by an additional $600 to keep her Safety Reserve flat at 6 months.

Investing purpose #2: Retirement Fund

At this point you must have understood how counting only on Public Welfare for your retirement is uncertain. Rules change all the time and Governments around the world are having a lot of difficulties dealing with the situation. It will certainly be a big challenge for the next generations.

Either way, the Government's job has never been to provide you with nice cruises and round the world trips in old age. It was only about avoiding a disaster and guaranteeing you a minimum income that could help you survive when you are no longer able to produce anymore.

The rest is, has always been, and will become more and more up to you. That is why it is critical to start building a retirement fund as soon as possible. Something able to complement the increasingly uncertain public welfare and securely maintain your standard of living in the future.

The sooner you start investing, the less effort you'll need due to the effect of compound interest.

For those who do not remember, compound interest is that thing of interest yielding interest over time. That is, an interest rate of 1% per month will not give you 12% in a year, but something around 12.7%. That's because, if you invest $100, at the end of the first month you will have $ 101. In the second month, instead of the interest on the $100 you initially put, interests are going to apply to the $101 and instead of $102, you will get $102.01.

Okay, I know that talking like this, it doesn't sound very attractive, but if you can make good use of the virtue of our little friends who have waited to eat the marshmallow, in the end, the effect of compound interest in the long run will be hearty.

Just to give you an idea, this same 1% per month applied for 20 years, instead of 240% (20 years x 12 months x 1%), will yield 989%.

Understanding the power of this, changes everything. This is what makes an investor! Albert Einstein defined compound interest as the 8th wonder of the world. Whoever understands the mechanism of compound interest earns it. Who does not, pays it.

I'm puzzled on how people complain so much about the high interest rates charged by banks. Of course, interest is very bad when it plays against you, but it is a great opportunity for those who save.

It's your choice.

As one Chinese proverb says (now it's a real Chinese proverb, I swear): when winds blow, some people build walls. Others, windmills.

This discussion of compound interest is essential. It fits in several different moments of this book, but here in this chapter, it is simply fundamental. To form a fund for retirement takes time and this is the essential fuel to activate the power of compound interest.

It is also important to bear in mind that the interest rate that matters in this case is the real interest rate, and by that I mean discounted from inflation.

You know that in 20 years, $100 will not be able to buy what it buys today. To plan your retirement, you should take this into account. Just use a projection of real interest, already discounted from inflation.

"But Riko, how can I guess how inflation will be in the future?"

Well, not even future interest rates. We simply can't, but you can use the current scenario as a premise and keep adjusting it over the years. Remember no one has a crystal ball but doing something about it is always better than using it as an excuse.

How much should I invest per month?

This is a more complex calculation. In addition to interest rate and inflation expectations for the future, it should take into consideration the age at which you wish to retire, the average retirement income, life expectancy, and an estimate of Public Welfare income.

In the US, Social Security pays benefits that are on average equal to about 40 percent of your pre-retirement earnings. You may also be able to estimate your benefits.

As it is impossible to cover each specific situation, here are some examples. Maybe one can be close to your situation. Imagine a 25-year-old man with average monthly expenses of $ 4,000. Let's say that he wants to retire at the age of 70 and expecting to live up to age of 92. Assuming he would receive around $2,000 from Social Security and a real interest rate (discounted from inflation) of 4% p. a., he would have to save around $240 per month in order to keep the same spending of $ 4,000 per month at retirement.

Considering the same criteria above for those who are 35 years old, retirement requires a monthly investment of $390. At age 45, it would be necessary, $700. And finally, at 55, it would take $ 1,450 per month.

Considering in all cases that these savings start entirely from zero with no resource invested yet for this purpose. The examples above may serve as a reference, but the main message here is that the later you start investing, the more effort will be needed.

For something more personalized, the service of a Certified Financial Planner may be interesting.

If your monthly expenses increase, it will be harder to keep them in retirement. It will require more effort. If you cannot get the interest promised, idem. If life expectancy increases, same thing. Everything counts. But the complexity of the account cannot stop you from preparing for one of the most important accounts you have to pay: the amount you owe to "yourself from the future".

And the clock is ticking. Every second that passes without investing is making it harder and harder.

How much time do I have to build this fund?

You have all your productive life to prepare for this, although nothing prevents you from saving all at once should the opportunity arise.

Investing purpose #3: Investments to increase your living standards

The Safety Reserve and the Retirement Plans focus on security. Both serve to maintain your current standard of living, one in the event of an unforeseen momentary break in the source of revenue, the other in retirement.

But to increase your living standards, the goal is completely different. It is to dare and risk in a reasonable way. The goal is to build financial assets capable of generating extra income in the future, and thus make it possible to improve your standard of living. Risk will be a key variable in this equation. Any asset is acceptable as long as there is a solid expectation of future return.

How much time do I have to build this?

Your entire life. The first step is to establish a good strategy. If you start from scratch, I'd say plan at least 5 years ahead until you start to count on some extra income.

Up ahead, when you start to enjoy what you have built, use only a portion of the actual income from these investments to increase your standard of living and let the other portion continue to grow.

Once your Safety Reserve is built, or at least well underway, turn your focus here, for your enrichment. That is what "paying yourself first" means. This is the fun part and the final part of the Planning. It's like the tip of an iceberg. You cannot get here without first going through all the previous steps of planning, controlling, and investing in security, stages that cannot be skipped.

How much should I invest per month?

The story of the 10% of Clason's book seems to have become a law. The book dates back to the 1920s and has since been repeated as a mantra. It's a good deal. After all, just think about it: from every 10 coins won, spending 9 and saving 1 doesn't look like much, right? So, 10% is something simple and easy to achieve, but 10% is just the minimum.

It is a bit subjective in the sense that it depends on a lot of things.

Just to illustrate, this question about how much investment was needed was once made to the former Brazilian soccer player named Deco, in an interview on the TV.

Deco's response was: we should save 70% of what we earn.

The presenters, of course, were startled. But for an athlete like him, saving 70% of his income seems to me quite reasonable and even admirable. Despite stratospheric salaries, an athlete's career ends early. While in most professions, we can count on working for something around 40 years, a soccer player usually receives good salaries for a maximum of 15 years. If he becomes accustomed to a very high standard of living during his active years, it will be very hard to keep it when he stops playing. And that is exactly what happens to many of them.

There is no magic number of how much to save that works equally well for everyone. It all depends on your age, professional situation and your ambition. It is up to you to decide that. These are the directions of your life and deciding this is one of the coolest parts of the Financial Planning.

It is the definition of the strategy.

You cannot promise a single solution that can serve everyone. I, for example, find an allocation of 50-25-25 interesting. 50% of one's revenue used for Recurring Expenses, 25% for Saving for Short and Medium Terms and 25% for long-term Investment. I find it balanced given it's an allocation divided equally between present and future, and between the future in the short / medium and long terms.

If you want to invest a higher percentage, but at the moment you cannot get anything beyond the 10%, my suggestion is to make a progressive allocation of investment. That is, in bands.

The higher your income in a given period, a higher allocation to invest should be the goal.

Example: If you normally earn $3,000 per month, and you can only allocate $300 per month (10% of your income) to investments, okay. But from there on, everything that surpasses the $3000 of income, 50% will be used for short- and medium-term savings and the other 50% will be invested. The recurring costs don't change.

It is doable.

It is as if the percentage of your income dedicated to investments worked as a progressive income tax rate. But instead of paying the Government, you pay yourself.

Don't forget that within the group "Investments", the three subgroups should be considered: Safety Reserve, Retirement Fund and Increase of Living Standards. The first two are almost fixed values, calculated practically and directly. The third is more of a subjective percentage.

So, if you decide to invest 20% of what you earn, this means that in order to calculate how much to invest to increase your standard of living, you must multiply your net income by 20% and subtract from this amount what has been allocated in Safety and Retirement Reserves.

Total investment = Safety Reserve + Retirement Fund + Invest. To generate additional income

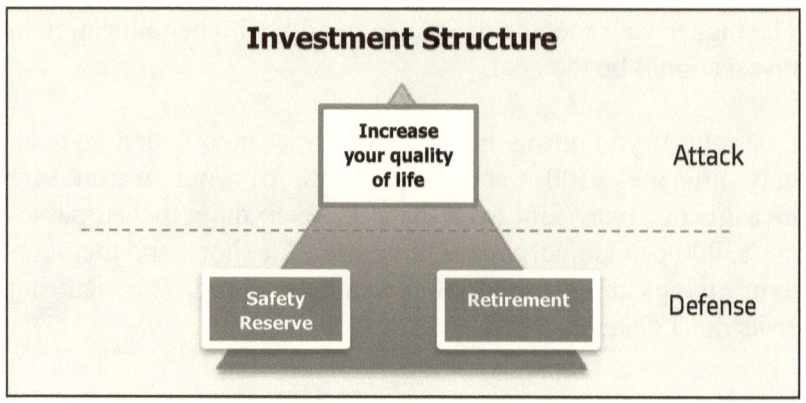

Now you may be thinking, "But how do I find money to pay the expenses of the month, savings for non-recurring expenses, putting together a Safety Reserve, a Retirement Plan and still invest to increase my income?"

Dude, just stop torturing yourself about it!

I know that for those who are not prepared, starting to think about all this at once is frightening, but all this is comprehensible and is part of everyone's life.

It's an everyday exercise, big changes don't happen all at once, they are performed little by little every day. It is challenging, I know but totally doable! A lot of people face their expenses by using debt. This makes the required effort infinitely greater. Just think about that! If you prepare properly, interest and other revenues will play in your favor. Save your time, money and energy by preparing properly and it could be hard for a while, but it will be way easier over time.

Even though right now you are possibly not fully prepared to meet all of these needs, getting to know them is an important step! As I said earlier on, once you have access to any extra revenue, you will know how to allocate it by having complete knowledge of your needs and goals.

It's amazing how people that have no idea of their needs spend what they shouldn't, throwing parties like P. Diddy, by feeling rich with the first sign of an additional income.

But guess what, in the end they always return to the same starting point!

The road is not easy. You've got to go up gradually. The light at the end of the tunnel will begin to shine and before you even realize it, you'll have already advanced a lot.

Start saving for all your goals and needs even if it is a symbolic value. I really mean a symbolic value. If all you can save now is $5. Do it! Think of it as just the first step. In the beginning, the habit is more important that the amount saved.

We always think we don't earn much. People like to imagine what they would do if they won the lottery. Everyone says they would invest and live only on the interest income. But why don't you do it right now with the income you have?

I always say that, who doesn't know how to live with little will not know how to live largely. Improvement should be a daily exercise. Those who see from afar may think that the rich are just lucky, but their wealth is the result of resilience, patience, discipline and constant overcoming.

Did you know that 80% of the people who win lottery prizes lose everything in up to five years and return to the same living standards they used to have before? It's incredible!

Others lose everything in a little longer time frame. It just shows how important it is for you to understand the value of the path. You will not be rich until you truly understand what being rich means.

It takes time to build something solid, but once it is built, it will be like a fortress. Beautiful and imposing, but also well protected.

CHAPTER TWENTY

Financial Products

An investment bank emailed my wife this week stating that she had a moderate profile.

Well, you know, my wife is dramatic, impulsive, bossy, euphoric, chatty, quarreling... she can be anything in this life, but if there is one thing which she is definitely not is moderate.

Seriously speaking, investment banks are required to send this type of questionnaire to their clients to define what they call the investor profile. It should basically determine the level of risk you're willing to take in exchange for high returns so you the bank can offer you the products that best fit your profile.

The results of this questionnaire can be: conservative, moderate or aggressive.

I have serious restrictions regarding the investment profile thing. To begin with, the way I see the world is not in black or white.

And I am not necessarily conservative, but I may find myself temporarily conservative now for a number of reasons such as not having a safety reserve, being in debt, or having lost my job. These things can prevent me from being more aggressive in investing. But that is temporarily.

Once I've done my homework and financial control is in place, I may become more aggressive. You can continue to read investment books; your knowledge of finance may increase, and your confidence will increase too.

Taking risks may even have a little to do with a certain profile, I agree but the main aspect here is, without a doubt, the moment in your financial life.

Someone who just got into a new, debt-ridden job with a lot of people who depend on him, with no Safety Reserve or anything I've shown here, no matter what his profile is, risk is not recommended for him. It is illogical. This is not the right time, you see it?

On the other hand, a young man who is feeling confident in his job and is up to date with his financial life, is totally ready for risk.

And I must confess, this risk universe is amazing. It really is something totally different, entirely apart.

But this risk appetite is not a natural "blessing" or "karma" that is simply born with the individual. Like any other characteristic, it is an achievement. It's like going through all the stages in a video game and it's time to face the big boss.

Each investor is living a moment in his life that is unique. It's about that moment, that phase.

People often ask me what the best investment is. I regret to disappoint them because the answer is far from being nice. The best investment depends on the reasons why you are saving that amount of money.

As we'll see, investing in the stock market is great for your long-term goals but a very bad idea for your short-term commitments. Ignoring this is the main reason why some people give up on investing and assume that one particular financial product is not good when maybe the issue is that this one product is not in line with the expectations.

You have to understand your needs first and then, place the correct amount in the correct box. It's like a game.

So far, we have talked about 4 main groups of saving, right? Just as a recap, we have seen:

1. Savings for short and mid-term expenses
2. Safety Reserve
3. Retirement Fund
4. Increase in Revenues

For each of these groups, you should invest in a different product.

Types of investment

There are two great types of investments: Fixed Income and Variable Income.

The first one is the kind of product in which by the time you invest your money you have a clear agreement of how much you are going to get back. It is mainly borrowings like regular Savings Accounts, Treasury Bonds, Company Bonds and so on. The most common type of earning of this type of investment is interest.

On the other hand, as the name suggests, in the Variable Income there is no such engagement. Stocks are considered Variable Income meaning that if you buy them, you'll earn a part of the Company's profit if there is any.

Variable Income investments are riskier in the sense that it is more volatile since there is no high engagement. But they also have higher expected returns that - if used correctly - can compensate for that additional amount of risk.

In order to put your different types of savings into the right boxes you will have to deal basically with 3 variables: liquidity, risk and expected return.

Because even if your goal is to maximize your returns, you wouldn't want to do that by risking your retirement or your safety reserve. Or imagine there is a big crisis like 1929 or 2008 and due to an economic recession, you lose your job and you also lose a big part of your investments because they were all in the stock market.

Liquidity is also a very important aspect. For those who do not remember, liquidity is the degree to which an investment can be quickly converted into cash, without losing much of its value.

Some kind of investments are only available in a certain date. Others are always available but selling them can cause high losses in their value. Those are considered investments with low liquidity.

For obvious reasons, cash is considered the most liquid asset, while real estate and fine art are relatively illiquid. Other financial assets, ranging from stocks to bonds, fall at various places on the liquidity spectrum.

The higher the liquidity, usually the lower the expected return is, but you still need it to meet your short-term commitments.

So, by managing correctly these three aspects of the investment products, we'll be able to better allocate our savings and build what we call an Investment Portfolio.

Below, there is a recap for the characteristics of a financial product we should value when deciding where to allocate our:

Investment objective	Risk	Liquidity	Return	Type of Investment
Savings for short and mid-term expenses	Low	High	Low	Fixed Income
Safety reserve	Low	High	Low	Fixed Income
Retirement fund	Low	Low	Medium	Mainly Fixed Income
Increase in Revenues	High	Low	High	Balanced Portfolio

Considering the characteristics of a good investment for each one of the 4, I would say that fixed income would be the most recommended for the first 3.

I believe the most important is the knowledge I'm passing here so that you are able to identify in every context which product will fit best the reason why you are investing. The economic environment is always changing and so is the financial market. So, for this reason, I see a lot more value in describing the characteristics of the good products that you should be looking for than just saying that you should invest in this or that and making you follow it with no idea of why you're doing it.

Nevertheless, as the nice guy I am, I'll also give my point of view with some examples of financial products I like. Don't take it as a financial advice, but as my personal opinion, based on what I do myself with my money.

For the savings for the short-term expenses, the best financial product would also be something practical and simple, available real time, and even if it changes from time to time and from country to country, and I'm sure you'll be able to recognize it in your own country. I, myself, use my **main bank's savings account**. Interest is not huge, but it doesn't have to be as the money will be coming and going. The objective here is to separate it from your checking account and, as a bonus, you can still earn something in terms of interest.

For savings for the mid-term expenses (the ones that will happen in more than one year), such as buying a new car or saving for a wedding party, **I like smaller online banks' CD (Certificate of Deposit)**, which are safe money you borrow to a bank and usually with higher returns than similar investments in large commercial banks. An online bank might pay three to five times the national average.

CDs are a safer and more conservative investment than stocks and bonds, offering lower opportunity for growth, but with a non-volatile, guaranteed rate of return. They generally pay higher interest rates than savings accounts, but whereas the latter allows you to vary your balance by making additional deposits, as well as up to six withdrawals per month, CDs require one initial deposit that stays in the account until it reaches its maturity date, whether that's six months or five years later. That's why it is best recommended for mid-term expenses.

But, although you lock into a term of duration when you open a CD, there are options for exiting early should you encounter an emergency or change of plans. I wouldn't recommend you rely on this, but it's good to know that the possibility exists.

What is a CD?

A certificate of deposit (CD) is a product offered by banks and credit unions that offers an interest rate premium in exchange for the customer agreeing to leave a lump-sum deposit untouched for a predetermined period of time. Almost all consumer financial institutions offer them, but its main characteristics such as term and interest vary from bank to bank.

They are one of the safest savings or investment instruments available, for two reasons: First, their rate is fixed and guaranteed, and Second, because the investment is also protected by the same federal insurance that covers all deposit products (FDCI/NCUA). When you open a CD with an FDIC- or NCUA-insured institution, up to $250,000 of your funds on deposit with that institution are protected by the U.S. government if that institution were to fail.

For the Safety Reserve, where security is the most important, I like Treasury bonds, which are the safest investment there is in any given Country. They are considered risk free because the guys you are lending your money to, are the same guys that own the money printer. So, if they run out of money, they can print more and pay you. It sounds nice, right? In the US, as liquidity is very important, **I'd say T-Bills**.

What is a T-Bill?

A Treasury Bill (T-Bill) is a short-term debt obligation backed by the U.S. Treasury Department with a maturity of one year or less. Therefore, it is considered the safest investment in the USA. In other words, to make it simple, when you buy a T-Bill, you are somehow lending money to the US Government.

 T-bills can have maturities of just a few days or up to the maximum of 52 weeks. The longer the maturity date, the higher tend to be the interest rate paid to the investor.

You can buy T-Bill in the secondary market through a broker, or you can access the website https://www.treasurydirect.gov/ (where you'll find plenty of interest information).

For retirement, in most countries, retirement plans benefit from tax relief. If you work for a Company that encourages its employees to invest by matching a certain amount, it is a great opportunity. So, if your Company offers **401k accounts**, max it out to the point where your company is matching the maximum. This is free money, man! Use it to buy funds that invest in long term debt.

Another good idea, if you don't work in a Company that matches your investments in 401k account, is to invest in long term Treasury Bonds, good, safe and usually with significant higher returns than the short-term ones. Which ones? The Inflation Protected ones, known as TIPS (Treasury Inflation-Protected Securities). Just go for the long-term ones (with maturity of up to 30 years). Open a Roth IRA account to invest in these Treasury Bonds and take advantage of the Tax Relief.

What are TIPS?

Treasury Inflation-Protected Security (TIPS) is a Treasury bond that is indexed to inflation (measured by the CPI) to protect investors from the negative effects of rising prices. The principal value of TIPS rises as inflation rises (or decreases in case of deflation). In addition, the investor receives interest every six months based on a fixed rate agreed upon at the moment of the purchase.

TIPS are issued with maturities of five, 10, and 30 years and are also considered a low-risk investment because the U.S. government backs them too. You can also buy them in the secondary market through a broker, or at https://www.treasurydirect.gov/. For retirement purposes, if your Company doesn't offer you any matches in 401k accounts, I strongly recommend you use your Roth IRA account for investing in TIPS.

Now, investing to generate additional revenues is the sexiest part of all that and in the next chapters, I will show you a good and simple strategy that anyone can apply in order to have good results in the long term with low risk.

Here is where we stand by now.

Investment objective	Risk	Liquidity	Return	In what I'd invest?
Savings for short-term expenses	Low	High	Low	Saving account of my main Bank
Savings for mid-term expenses	Low	Mid-High	Low	CD of an online bank
Safety reserve	Low	High	Low	Government Bonds (T-Bills)
Retirement fund	Low	Low	Medium	Long-Term Fixed Income Fund (through 401k ac.) or TIPS through Roth IRA
Increase in Revenues	High	Low	High	let's see in the next chapters…

CHAPTER TWENTY-ONE

Investing has to be simple

Modesty aside, no one I know is better in bets than me. I feel very comfortable to say that because I've been addicted to sporting bets - especially soccer games - since college, and that only increased when I began my professional life.

As I work with finance and there is always people willing to play! In my first internship, we used to bet absolutely everything you can imagine, and the track record has always been very positive for me.

I didn't win all bets, sure, but I won a lot more often than I lost. Even in defeats, I was usually very close to winning until the end.

The reason why I'm saying all this is not to brag about a kind of natural talent for predicting the future, but to explain something very simple. Really, very, very simple!

Although I have always been a huge soccer fan since I was a kid, that's definitely not what helped me and honestly, from my experience, often, this is usually even more harmful.

Just think about the bets at work at the last Soccer World Cup, if you have participated in one. Who won it? Let me tell you one thing, 90% of the time, the person who wins World Cup bets are people that have no idea of who the players in each team are. Don't want to be politically incorrect, but usually girls who never watch any kind of sports and just play for fun, do very well.

Why is that? Betting is purely luck?

No. It is purely statistics!

And without noticing it, most of us are very bad at statistics.

The problem is that in trying to predict, we usually overestimate the value of the stories and undervalue the numbers. We tend to bring to the bets an unnecessary complexity that ends up hindering rather than helping.

Most of my friends that used to play sport bets with me all the time were 100% tuned to team news and therefore, their bets were totally biased with so much unneeded information. Then they used to come up with ideas like "I think team Z is going to lose because Crazy John is injured," or "this nontraditional team is good and will be a surprise playing away because the other team is not expecting them to be so good".

I do not.

My bets have always been: the favorite wins. Always. When in doubt of who the favorite is, by bet was: the home team wins.

The results I used to bet were limited to the following options: 2×1 or 1×0 (0x0 or 2×0 only when I wanted to be extravagant!). For those not aware, these are the most recurring scores in soccer games.

So far, there is no magic. Just keeping it as simple as possible.

Where is the problem then? Well, everyone knows that the favorites do not always win and that in almost every round there are some unexpected results. This is what usually happens in real life. Everyone knows that and because they know it, most people try to guess what the surprise of the round will be.

Big mistake!

As the name implies, surprise is an unlikely event. It is difficult to predict it. I don't risk it. I am aware that out of the 10 games in the round, I will usually hit an average of 7. Sometimes more, sometimes less.

My opponents, trying to guess what these "3 surprises" will be, eventually fall short because the probability of hitting surprises is very low. And not only that. When they believed that one team was way better than the other, they would bet a high score such as 3 x 0 or 4 x 1.

I would never do that! Because even if they are right about high scores, there are so many options that they'll probably miss the right one. It could be 5 x 0, 6 x 2... 7 x 1 (no need to comment about the later).

Even if he thinks the game will be a thrashing, he will hardly hit the score. Chances are way higher to hit the scoring of a tighter game.

As a result, not all rounds I win, but I am frequently among the highest scorers and as the Championship goes, I distance myself with probably the simplest strategy of all.

Statistically, the name of this is "regression to the mean". That is, without actual data that really impacts the result, the best guess is the historical average. There is one reason why favorites are considered favorites: they have more chances to win.

The problem is that our mind believes more stories with cause-effect relationships than in pure statistics. We always try to seek justifications from a cause that can even be real, but that will not necessarily be strongly related to the result.

We feel that results need to be justified by stories. A sports commentator will be saying the next day that the favorite team lost because the player NJ did not play. But if the team wins, the same fact can be used in favor.

It is always easy to explain results after.

You'll never see a commentator saying: the favorite team has lost because statistically it is proven that in 30% of games the favorites lose for whatever reason.

The reason why I am saying all this is because it happens in the exact same way in the Financial Market. If a minister makes an important speech, this fact will be used to justify both the fall or the rise of the British Pound on the day, whether or not the news actually impacted the exchange rate.

But we buy this news and more than that, we tend to give it more weight than it would be justified statistically.

And when statistics come in, things get even worse.

Gambling

A few years ago, I was once playing the lottery - without much patience to pick the numbers because I know there is not much chance of winning – when I had a small discussion with one of my workmates.

Before I continue, I have to say I don't like playing lottery games, but sometimes I do it just to socialize.

I like betting when I actually have control of my bet and real chances of winning. The lottery is not it. Anyone who understands the minimum of statistics knows that the odds are 0.0% in our favor.

There is a possibility, but no probability.

And still, people play it.

Going back to the day I was picking numbers with no patience. My final bet was: 1, 2, 3, 4, 5 and 6.

One of my friends who was organizing the bet said that I was kidding him. He said my combination was impossible just because I had chosen 6 sequential numbers. He said: "This is never going to happen!" and I replied, "I know. But it's not going to be yours either. Want to bet about that?"

It's not impossible to win, but the rounded probability of hitting lottery's big prize is negligible. And the odds of hitting my 6 numbers were as probable as any other combination. Any other!

And that is the trick our minds play on us.

Since lottery numbers are usually non sequential, by opting for random non sequential numbers, the guy feels that he is closer to winning, even if he is not.

He has the illusion that the combination he chooses is more likely to come out because it looks more realistic.

Only there are millions of such combinations.

And this is the exact same mistake that my friends from sports betting used to make when they included surprises in their bets. It gave them the illusion that their bets were more coherent because their combination of results looked more like results that normally happen.

Regression to the mean. This is the best way to be closer to the result.

Consider the following test with 2 independent questions:

I want you, without further information, to guess a person's nationality.

1) If you had to guess if he is Chinese or not. What would you choose?

2) And now guess his nationality.

Well, let me tell you what my answers would be: for the first one, I would say that the person is not Chinese. For the second question, my answer would be: The person is Chinese.

Although the 2 answers seem contradicting, in reality, they are not.

The best answer is always the most likely option, and as far as I know, there is at least 4 times more chance of not being Chinese than of being (considering that the Chinese population is about 1/5 of the global population).

Whereas, for the second question, I know that China is the most populous country on planet and that the chances are greater of being Chinese than any other nationality if considered individually.

And with my choices I'd still leave the game with 1 point guaranteed, since one of the 2 questions I will surely get right.

Depending on the number of test takers (and, of course, luck), I might not even win because someone lucky can get both answers correct, which I can't, as well as not winning every round of the jackpot. But if this kind of challenge continues, whoever is lucky in this round is unlikely to keep being lucky in future rounds and who opts for statistics rather than guessing will eventually overtake him at some point.

The problem with people as they overvalue stories rather than statistics is that a guy who is not Chinese in the first question cannot change his nationality in the second question. He either is or is not Chinese. When the questions are asked, they create a character in their minds. They focus on the story rather than in the game.

How does this translate to the financial market?

Just as my friends think they can guess what the upset of the next round will be, so do active investors who believe they can figure out what the next Google will be in the stock market.

By the time Google came into existence, thousands of other start-ups appeared around the world, particularly in the US, and looked very promising. The financial market bought into the idea in the late 1990s until the dam burst in 2000, what became known as the dotcom bubble. Most of those start-ups didn't make - and never made - any profits. Some went bankrupt.

Among them, Google resisted and grew into one of the largest companies on the planet.

The chances of you knowing back in the 90's that Google would become what it has become today would be like looking for a needle in a haystack of thousands of other start-ups. Would it be possible for the individual investor to identify the champion within that scenario?

Possible yes, but again, very unlikely. The most likely result of this type of bet is that you would have lost a lot of money by betting on other start-ups that would sink halfway.

But the funniest thing about all of these cases is that you don't think they apply to you.

You believe you are able to pick the right stock, the results on the sport bets and the lottery numbers like all Casino gamblers get into the table certain they'll win.

Researchers Van Yperen and Buunk back in 1991 called this effect as the Illusory Superiority, a cognitive dysfunction that makes us overestimate our abilities.

10 years earlier, a survey by Svenson showed that 93% of American drivers believed they drove better than average. The same kind of test was done several times and the results were very similar: most people believe their IQ is above average, most

children believe they are better than average, and most workers believe they are more productive than average.

If we had a closer idea of reality, the result of these tests would be close to 50%. Any small variation could be justifiable, but that's not the case. We overestimate our capacities.

That is why we hear inexperienced investors asking what the best investment in the market is.

> *"Number one rule of Wall Street. Nobody… and I don't care if you're Warren Buffet or if you're Jimmy Buffet. Nobody knows if a stock is gonna go up, down, sideways or in fucking circles. Least of all, stockbrokers, right?* (Mark Hanna in The Wolf of Wall Street by Jordan Belfort)

A Cass Business School test showed that between 1968 and 2011 monkeys chose better stocks than financial market professionals. Another study showed that 96% of mutual funds failed to hit the market within 15 years.

The result? You pay all these investment fees to have a horrible result. It is expensive to try to beat the market. The stock picking strategy requires time, energy and, of course, money.

For some years I worked as an Investor Relations Specialist. Our role is to inform and clarify any questions the market may have about the Company. Investors from all around the world call us, read our reports and talk to the board to understand the Company's strategy.

Some come on-site to visit stores, all to gain an understanding of how business works and to gauge whether the stock is worth investing in or not.

But this process is very expensive. These guys who move around, stay in nice hotels, go to fine restaurants, move from meeting to meeting in taxis, and travel on business class. And their salary is really not bad.

Now, do you know who pays for it? Investors of active funds do.

All this to have a 50% chance to outperform the market.

No, wait a minute, let me rephrase it: all this to have a good story to tell.

Illusory Superiority!

All they do is create stories. Don't get me wrong, they believe in their stories, and honestly, most of the time they are not even wrong in their judgement.

The problem is not that they are false, but that they overvalue the weight of these stories. And they charge a high price for doing so.

Hitting the market is not hard, the hard thing is consistently hitting the market year after year. This is hard. Guys like Warren Buffet and Ray Dalio have done it, but what are the chances of you finding one of them on your way?

Other guys could do it, but listen, like Tony Robbins once said, if we pack 1024 gorillas in a gymnasium and give each one a coin to flip 10 times, one of them would flip heads 10 times in a row. It's pure statistics, so when this happens, you call it luck. But in the financial market, you call the guy a genius.

What I mean is that the best strategy for an individual investor is to invest in the market as a whole. You can use regression to the means in your investment strategy. People usually hate to be average, we simply love to feel naturally special.

Don't be afraid of the average. It won't bite you.

Quite the opposite, to be honest. This way you can diversify your portfolio and reduce your costs. This type of strategy is cheap because it avoids the costs of having a team investigating reports and traveling to find hot news. Ultimately, an Excel macro would be enough to buy and sell the stocks that make up an index.

Most funds that seem to over perform on the market, in reality, don't do it. When we discount the costs incurred during the year, their performance is actually worse.

My strategy is very simple: Don't even try to guess. Simply replicate the market using index funds as a reference. The world economy is growing and as a result, new companies offering new products are born every day. They come with new solutions for society and new opportunities for profit growth. There is a constant evolution going on and this trend is very unlikely to change in the future.

Warren Buffet addressed this subject in one of his recent reports explaining how population growth and extraordinary gains of productivity will create an enormous increase in wealth for the next generations. That has already been the case for at least the last 300 years.

Buy the market instead of picking stocks. Be active in your life and passive in your investment strategy. It will save you a lot of time and energy with fair financial results. The problem with this strategy is that it is very simple, and people don't like simplicity. They are willing to pay big money to hear complex jargons, people dressed in nice suits with colorful graphs in a 4-screen desktop. They want to learn how to read graphs so they can spend their last dime on brokerage fees buying and selling stocks as if from one minute to the other, the entire world had changed and a stock that was worth holding two minutes ago, is not worth anymore.

Complexity, that is what they want.

And if that is what they value, I'll try to defend my position then using other words just to satisfy them.

CHAPTER TWENTY-TWO

Building a portfolio that generates additional revenue

In this chapter I'll allow myself to be a little more technical. The main message is the same as the one from the previous chapter, I will simply detail it a little better.

So, before I deep dive into the investment strategy, I will make a recap of the 2 main types of assets, one should hold in his or her portfolio.

A few words about Stocks & Bonds

Stocks and bonds represent two different ways for a Company to raise money to fund or expand its business.

When a company issues stock, it sells to someone a piece of itself. The new stockholder (or shareholder) will become one of the owners of that Company, having the right to vote in important matters of the Company in the Shareholdings Meetings and also receive a part of the Company's profit. The part of the Company's annual profit that is distributed is called dividend. Each shareholder receives a part of the dividend that is proportional to the share it has over the total Company. So, if you own 0.5% of the total amount of stocks of a particular entity, you'll receive 0.5% of the total amount of dividends distributed.

Most people think that the only way to make money in the stock market is by buying at low prices and selling at high. But this is only one way to make money. It is called capital gains. Another possibility is to keep the hen of the golden eggs with you. Don't sell it and you'll be entitled to receive a portion of that Company's profit forever. It's a bit like buying a house. You can do it to sell it right away with some financial gains, or you can keep it and receive rent in return.

Not all companies distribute dividends, it's worth saying. Some of them decide to reinvest the entire annual profit in order to increase the business. But a shareholder would benefit from that too because as the business grows, the value of the stock he holds tends to grow too as long as the Company is in financial health.

On the other hand, when an entity issues a bond, it is issuing debt with the agreement to pay interest for the use of the money.

I know every time we say there is debt involved, most people tend to think of banks. This is only half true. The market for bonds works in a very similar way of the one of stocks. Investors buy these bonds and decide to carry them in exchange of receiving interest instead of dividends. The price of the bonds also fluctuates in the market, meaning that you can also buy a bond a resell it with capital gain (or loss). Obviously, the volatility is a lot lower than the stock market because bonds are safer securities. First, because there is usually no change in the return for a bond that depends on the Company performance. Interest is pre-defined so, even if the Company's profit skyrocket, the return of bonds shouldn't change. Second of all, the risk is lower, since the Stockholder is the last one to receive anything in case of a Company liquidation. Not only companies issue bonds. Government and financial institution also do.

To make it short, for the investor's perspective, what is important to know is that bonds tend to be safer assets while stocks offer higher expected returns. Both are available for investors to buy.

Risk vs. Return

When we talk about good investments for the future, there is nothing but hopes about what is going to happen. There is always a risk that these expectations are not confirmed.

The return of some assets doesn't vary much from what is expected. Some others' varies a lot. And this is the definition of risk in the financial market: how much an asset's return varies from what is expected.

Controlling risks is a key element when building a portfolio. Buying assets without assessing its risks is like going for a picnic without checking the weather forecast. Everything can be alright in a given weekend, but if you plan to have one picnic every week, you better take care.

The problem is that everyone prefers assets that present a certain stability with lower risks and in the end, as a result of supply x demand relation, the riskier assets present highest expected returns.

What do you do, then?

Not easy, right?

Your goal in this game is to both maximize the returns and minimize the risks of your portfolio.

And the best way to assess this relation between risk and return is by simply calculating the amount of expected return for every percentage of risk.

Again, just to simplify it, a quality of an asset is given in the following formula:

$$\frac{Expected\ Return}{Risk}$$

This very simple and intuitive formula gives us the basis for what is called the Sharpe Ratio. It divides the expected return of an asset by its risk using projected information based most of the time on historical data.

And of course, the higher the return per unit of risk, the better the investment is.

Just to give you a very simple example, let's say that the Google shares (Alphabet Inc.) offer 15% of expected return and 30% of volatility in the year. This means that a simplified Sharpe Ratio would be of 0.5 (15% / 30%).

Why do I call it "simplified" Sharpe Ratio? Because for the regular Sharpe Ratio we should also include the concept of a Risk-Free asset, that, as the name says, are assets that present no risk.

A good proxy of a Risk-Free asset in the US would be the Government Bonds known as T-Bill (the same one I said I liked for Saferty Reserve, remember?).

So, the original Sharpe Ratio would give you the expected Return of an asset in addition to the return of a Risk-Free asset per every amount of risk.

$$Sharpe\ Ratio = \frac{(Return\ of\ the\ asset - Return\ of\ Risk\ Free\ Asset)}{Risk\ of\ the\ given\ asset}$$

All figures are based on expectation only.

Do I sound very technical? If you thought "yes", please don't be afraid of it. The idea is just to simplify these financial concepts.

So, Riko, does it mean that I should just measure that and pick the stock that presents the highest Sharpe ratio and invest it all in that stock?

No. That is not my point!

Let me finish and you'll see how it works.

There is a magic word that I haven't talked about yet and it is called "diversification".

You know grandma used to say don't put all your eggs in one basket? It's the same, only explained in a fancier way.

Let the time of glamour begin…

Before I continue, there is a concept that I'd like to explain better. I've been most of the time referring to Risk as volatility, correct? Why? Because that volatility is what creates uncertainties in the future price of the asset. A statistician would say that "risk is the standard deviation from the expected return". I think this definition could be simplified with an example.

Going back to our Google example, with the Expected Return of 15% and a Risk of 30%. What would that mean in a very simple world? If would mean that we would expect Google Stock prices to vary from -15% to +45% given its volatility of 30%:

15% of expected return "+" and "-" 30% of Risk

The magic is that when you add a second asset to your portfolio, your Sharpe Ratio is very likely to improve even if that second asset is worse than the first one.

Coming back to our Google stocks example with a 0.5 Sharpe ratio. Let's say that Netflix, on the other hand, has expected return of 10% per year and risk of 25%, therefore, a simplified Sharpe Ratio of 0.25. At first by taking only this simplified Sharpe Ratio approach, Netflix looks worse, right?

But by combining them in the same portfolio, you could have an expected return of 12.5% and risk of also 12.5% and a Sharpe ratio of 1 which is better than the Sharpe Ratio of any of your stocks when analyzed in a stand-alone basis.

If you add a third stock, you're likely to improve even more your portfolio's risk-return relation. And the same idea is true for the fourth, fifth and so on.

Why is that?

You know, when we combine different assets in one portfolio, their expected return is averaged but the risk is lowered. The magic word that makes the risk go down when you include more stocks in your portfolio is "correlation".

In other words, the lower the correlation between different stocks, the better the effect will be of combining them in the same portfolio because in that way, risks will be diluted.

For example, if you find 2 stocks in which their correlation is negative, it means that when one is underperforming its expected return, the other one will be likely overperforming it, overall offsetting a great part of your portfolio risk.

This happens because stocks react differently to changes in the economic environment. For example, if oil prices go down, this will be bad news for Companies from the Oil & Gas Industry, but they could have a very positive impact in the airline market. Because for the Oil & Gas companies, a drop in the price of oil decreases their revenues, while for airlines, it will reduce their costs. Bad for ones, good for others. This is what negative correlation means.

So, if you have stocks with at least a low correlation, the risk of one will be partially offset by the behavior of the other.

So, as long as you have low correlations among the stocks and positive Sharpe Ratio of each of them, combining different stocks in your portfolio will be healthy for the risk return relation of your portfolio.

"Riko, when you said it would be easy, I wasn't expecting all that"

I know, I know, but trust me. I am not telling you to go out there and analyze all stocks, check "expected returns", "risks", "correlations", or any of these. No! I just want to make you see what I see. I want you to understand the power of diversification in boosting the amount of expected return over a certain amount of risk in a portfolio.

It's just the general idea that I want you to get here.

And I recognize a very import point about it: for the average investor, opening such a large group of different stocks is definitely not even efficient because even though it looks great in theory, when it comes to real life, if you try to do that, you will face very high brokerage fees and it will be very hard for you to have control over such a large portfolio. It is inefficient.

What to do, then?

A-ha! Glad you asked…

ETF

ETF is an acronym that stands for Exchange Traded Funds, in other words, they are funds traded on the stock exchange as if they were stocks.

The difference is that when you buy an ETF, you are not buying a single stock, but a portion of a nice and well diversified portfolio. This allows you to maximize your portfolio's Sharpe ratio no matter how small the amount you invest.

The advantage of investing in an ETF versus a traditional fund is that management fees are infinitely smaller. It is especially an advantage for investors who want to keep investing in the long run.

But how can these ETFs charge such small fees?

To answer it, I will have to go back and talk about the difference between the passive and the active strategies, the two basic strategies to decide how to invest.

In the active strategy, the goal is to outperform the market, while in the passive, the investor understands how difficult it is to outperform the market and how doing so increases the investments risk. Therefore, he decides to simply replicate the performance of the total market.

Why would you choose to replicate the market if you could try to beat it?

It is simple, remember my friends for the Sports bet? Most people just won't beat the market in the long run no matter how hard they believe they can.

All the professional investors – some of them with many years of experience in the field - wake up every day in search of the stocks that are going to bomb in the market. These guys spend a lot of time studying, reading Company's Financial Statements, following up the news and interviewing with Company's managers trying to understand their strategies. And of course, for all that effort, these teams get very well paid for all the work they do.

But on the other hand, passive funds are a lot easier to manage. You don't need a full team of well-educated MBA analysts nor travel nor meetings with CEOs. You don't even need to spend time with Bloomberg or the Financial Times subscription. All you have to do is copy the index you refer to. If it is the S&P 500, you would just have to make sure your portfolio has all the stocks in the same proportion as the index itself.

Passive funds are shortcuts.

You assume that all you need to do is trust that the market will do a good job on asset pricing as a whole. A big index like S&P

500 is a good proxy of the whole US market and the market performance represents the average of every investor's choice.

It means that using a passive approach, you will take advantage of every choice an active investor makes. But the beauty of it all is that to achieve the market result you will save all that time, effort and money that active investors spend trying to beat the market. An effort that will not pay off for at least half of them.

It is simple, cheaper, safer and wise to just follow. By not trying to beat the market you will never be under it either. Your performance will be the market! Nothing more, nothing less. And no extravagant administration or performance fees.

As a shareholder of an ETF index fund, you own part of the cash flow generated by a long list of different companies that are on that index. It means that the Global economy is working for you while you sleep. Definitely not a bad deal, isn't it?

If your goal is to retire and relax in your swimming pool at home without stressing so much about ups and downs in stock prices on a daily basis or even just focus on your profession and invest in your free time, go passive. Buy ETF and let the market work for you. It's the best deal I know even in terms of Sharpe Ratio. By averaging different Expected Returns with a level of Risk highly diluted with a diversified portfolio you maximize the return of your portfolio with a low level of risk.

Should I just buy ETFs and that's it?

Think of this: The economy is made of cycles, every 20 years there is usually a crash in the Financial Markets, and there is a crisis somewhere in the Globe that is going to affect all the other economies. It happened in Russia in 1998, in Asian Emerging markets in 1997, in 1999 it was the Long-Term Capital Management – the largest hedge fund of all times - that collapsed. And then there was WorldCom and Enron, the 9/11, Iraq and Afghanistan wars and a whole lot of other not so good-looking events ending up with the famous and most significant crisis of our time: the 2008 financial crisis, which still runs today's news and behaviors.

In all these different periods, the stock market has gone down but always recovering some time later. In the long run, despite many short-term setbacks, the stock market typically rises because the world economy expands, companies become more profitable, and the workers become more efficient and productive as a result of better education and new technologies.

You, I and a lot of other individuals wake up every single day trying to make a difference, to build a better future. We don't always realize it, but we are all creating new processes, enhancing knowledge and bringing improvement somehow. They seem very tiny, but we are billions of people doing it all the time. Well, maybe except for some Sundays.

And we know from our personal lives that things do not always work as they should, and we usually overvalue unexpected results. But if you look at the big picture, normally, it pays off. The trend is very positive.

I know history doesn't repeat itself, but it rhymes. There is a lot we can learn from the past.

So, to sum up, we know that the stock market reflects economical behavior and follows its general upward trajectory; that corrections happen regularly, and no one can predict exactly how and when they are going to happen; the market usually rebounds quickly resuming its positive long-term trend.

The question now is how to make these cycles work for you on an auto pilot.

The answer is: by having a balanced portfolio with both Fixed Income and ETFs.

It is a very simple and efficient strategy. Let's say you have a portfolio composed with 50% of the total investment allocated in ETFs and 50% in Bonds. All you have to do is to adjust your portfolio every quarter in order to keep that 50-50 balance.

What happens when the stock markets skyrocket and your portfolio now is made of 70% ETF and only 30% in Bonds?

You will be forced to rebalance it by selling that 20 extra percentage points of ETFs and use that amount to buy Bonds in order to readjust your portfolio with the desired balance.

If instead, a temporary crisis turns it into 35% ETF and 65% Bonds, you then would have to sell Bonds and buy the equivalent amount in ETF to keep the 50%-50% balance.

What I find beautiful about that very simple strategy is that you will always be forced to sell stocks when the stock market is high and to buy them when they are low, making the economic cycles work for you.

This is completely the opposite of what the great majority of investors do. Even if we all know that the goal is to buy stocks when they are cheap and sell them when they are expensive, in reality, investors tend to simply inverse it all by buying stocks when they are rising and sell them when they are low valued. This is simply the best strategy to lose money easily and quickly.

A balanced portfolio with Bonds and ETFs is a structured simple way to always be on the right side and looking at the long-run.

It's automatic. It saves you energy and time. No need to be an expert. No need to calculate Sharpe Ratio. No need to check Bloomberg, to talk to the Investor Relations guys, etc. And yet, you'll be doing what guys like Jack Bogle, Warren Buffet, David Swensen and Ray Dalio would tell you to do.

Maybe your bank manager will advise you otherwise because, you know, they need to sell their costly funds with high management fees. And brokerage houses will try to sell you incentives to trade stocks as much as you can, even offering you free courses of how to turn you into the best day trader in the world. It looks so nice to be a trader, but in reality, what they want is the outrageous brokerage commission. They just love when their clients trade a lot, they lure you in and hook you with ads of free or low-cost trade fees along with market insights that will help you choose the winners. Just like a good Casino in Las Vegas would offer you free drinks so that you gamble with them.

But, keep that in mind: the house always wins.

How much of each asset should I have in my balanced portfolio?

Stocks are the best investments for the long-run because even if they represent a high amount of risk, they tend to increase over time reflecting the economies advances that we have just discussed above. Consequently, bonds are recommended for shorter term investments because they are safer.

Therefore, the younger you are, the higher the stock stake of your total portfolio and of course, the older you are, the less you will be able to take advantage of the long-term impact over stocks.

A simple way to balance your portfolio is called the Life-Cycle strategy adjusting the proportion of each asset according to your age, i.e. slowly increasing the portion of bonds while you are aging.

I suggest that when you are 20 years old and you have all the long-term opportunities ahead you, you should invest 100% of your portfolio in stocks. Every year, you should increase the portion of your fixed income by 2%, so that when you are 30, and probably receiving considerably more money than when you were at 20, you would allocate 20% of your investments in Fixed Income and 80% in stocks.

If you follow this rule, in your 70 years old birthday party, you should be telling your friends that you have just moved your entire portfolio to safer short-term investments like Bonds.

Of course, you don't have to stick to this rule to the penny. Actually, in order to make it easier to follow, I suggest you give your investments a 5-percentage point's allowance.

So, if they should be at 20%-80% and they are currently around 23%-77%, it is okay. Otherwise, you risk losing a lot of money in transactions costs such as brokerage fees.

Age	Fixed Income	Variable Income
20	0%	100%
25	10%	90%
30	20%	80%
35	30%	70%
40	40%	60%
45	50%	50%
50	60%	40%
55	70%	30%
60	80%	20%
65	90%	10%
70	100%	0%

A very good way of rebalancing little deviations in your portfolio is to adjust your monthly investments avoiding buy and sell expenses as much as you can.

But at the same time, you have to be firm, and adjust if the percentages surpass that allowance. Using the 20%-80% example, if they ever reach 30%-70% you will have to rebalance them to realign your goal, so you must have the 20%-80% in end. It will help you adjust less in the future and take advantage of the selling-high and buying-low strategy.

In which ETF should I invest?

As ETFs are already well diversified, look for ones with low fees and that represent the market better. I like the idea of holding 2 ETFs representative of the market: one domestic, in the US linked to the S&P500 and another one Global that would also benefit of the safety of developed countries in Europe and Japan, and especially the potential growth in the Emerging ones like China and India.

And in which Bonds should I invest?

Corporate Bonds will give you higher returns and higher risk than Treasury Bonds. You can also include some Municipal Bonds if you want. The great news is that there are also ETF for this kind of Bonds so, all you have to do is to apply everything I just said about ETFs of stocks to ETFs of Bonds and you'll be all set.

I found it very interesting all you just said, but I prefer a simpler approach...

I love finance and investing and that's the reason why I chose it for my life. You can see me as a weirdo but thinking about asset allocation excites me and I know it also does for some other people.

Others won't feel the same, though. I know that. If that's your case, and you liked what I just described but doesn't want to commit to balancing your portfolio every quarter, you can invest in a Lifecycle or Target Date fund (they both mean the same thing). Basically, what these funds do is really close to everything I have just described in detail. So, if you opt to invest in a fund like this, you should be just fine even if paying somebody else to do the rebalancing job for you. It is really up to you.

So...

To sum-up, my aim here is to show you how to create the best portfolio that is return-risk balanced in a way that will save you a lot of time on research and ineffectual effort.

If you follow these simple rules, you will likely be safe and achieve high goals in your financial life, by using smart and reasonable shortcuts.

But attention: you should use the Life-Cycle strategy for your investments to increase your income, not for Safety Reserve for example.

Now, it might be a good time for a recap,

- Your priority number 1 is to create savings for your Short-Term Expenses.
- Then, start creating a Safety Reserve of at least the equivalent of 3 months of your average expenses (usually, the best for most people is 6 months). Once, you achieve at least one third of your final objective for the Safety Reserve, you can keep saving in a slower pace until you achieve the ideal amount. Invest it all in a safe short-term investment.
- Save for your retirement in order to keep the same standard of life you have today by picking long-term safe investments.
- Once you have at least 1/3 of your Safety Reserve and you are in the right path regarding your retirement plan, start investing to create extra revenue. For this, create a Life-Cycle Balanced Portfolio with a small number of well diversified ETFs of Stocks and Bonds.

In the meantime, don't forget your short-term needs and goals and be prepared for them.

Below, the table now completed:

Investment objective	My favorite investment
Savings for short-term expenses	Savings account of my main Bank
Savings for mid-term expenses	CD of online banks
Safety reserve	Government Bonds (T-Bills)
Retirement fund	Long-Term Fixed Income Fund through 401k account or TIPS through Roth IRA
Increase in Revenues	Balanced Portfolio ETF of Stocks and ETFs of Bonds or Target Date Funds

CHAPTER TWENTY-THREE

Real Estate

Most people dream of buying their own property someday. Reasons vary. Among the most popular are the incorrect beliefs that real estate prices always go up over time and that rent is money thrown in the trash.

Trying to demystify these myths, several economists have sought to clarify these points for the general public.

Regarding the idea that real estate only appreciates over time, let's go to the simple fact that… hmm, **they just don't**.

The 2008 crisis is a great example of that, and it is definitely not the only one. There is no certainty and it will never be that in the future Real Estate prices are always going to go up. But honestly it shouldn't stop us from investing in it, right? After all, stock prices don't always go up either.

Others see rent as if they were throwing money away. I will never understand that. I guess that for these people buy food and travel are also to through money away. Ultimately, every expense they must see it this away. Let me tell you one thing, rent is not a waste of money. For everything in life, there is a cost, so is housing. And buying your own property is a cost as well. It's the grand opportunity cost.

Enough of blablabla, let me tell you a story about my friend Lilly, who was 27 when she came to me looking for advice. The apartment she wanted to rent, she learnt that it was also for sale, whatever came first. The price they were asking for the apartment was $400 thousand. For rent, they were asking for $1,200 a month. She was excited to buy, because she had been granted from her bank an amount of mortgage equivalent to 80% of the total price of the apartment and if she put down $80 thousand (that by the way she had most of it and her parents would help with the rest), she would pay less than $2,000 a month to have her own apartment. For less than $800 a month, she could buy instead of spending that money renting it. She was very excited, and I never say anything in this kind of situations, especially when you see that the person is so excited about something like she was. So, I was just bouncing my head sharing her excitement. I ordered beers to celebrate the great conquer it was for her to buy her own property, and, so young, it was a high achievement! Everybody excited sharing the joy.

But them she turned to me and naively said "what do you think?". That question completely moved the tone of the conversation to another level. Suddenly, the whole place appeared to have become darker, my eyes of a good friend, happy to share joy with my friend, turned into something a lot more obscure. She awakened the economist that lives inside of me. And people tend to think that we, the economists, are stubborn, self-centered, arrogant, cold, and we see ourselves as omniscient beings… I agree with them.

So, I started to walk her through my thoughts. I said that she could also invest her $80,000 in a financial asset instead, where, at that time, she could receive around 5% a year for that. Then, she could do the same for the almost $800 a month that she would save if she preferred to rent rather than buy, by paying 1,200 as rent instead of the almost 2,000 of mortgage. In the end of the same 30 years period when she would have finished paying her mortgage and the apartment would finally be hers, if she decided for rent-and-invest instead, she would have one million dollars.

And I'm just simplifying things right here – I continued – as you mentioned that the $80,000 is all you currently have, what would you do in case you faced an emergency? What if you lose your job? Most people think that by buying a house they are being conservative, but if that is your only investment, how diversified you think your portfolio is? And that additional $800 a month that you'll put in, will it be used for diversification? Nooo.

And I'm just being nice because when you own a property, you become responsible for costs such as structural maintenance and property tax that when you rent you usually don't have to pay. And when you buy your house, you think you are buying a $400,000 one, right? But you are not! Actually, you have to pay commission to an agent; for your mortgage, there will be several different kinds of fees and insurances. In some states, they'll charge you a fee required for recording and holding the information regarding the sale with your county register of deeds, the State Recording Fees. All this is usually hidden from you when people say their property has increased X% in value of the years.

Even though some properties can be real good investments, Nobel Prize Robert Shiller found that from 1890 and 2019, home prices have increased a poor 0.6% a year in average (after accounting for inflation). Just to compare, the average real return of the S&P500 in the same period was 7% per year.

She was looking at me as if she wanted me dead in fire like Joan of Arc, but for some minutes I didn't care, or… the economist inside me didn't care. Actually, he rarely cares, to be honest. I knew a transformation was about to take place and that in the end she would realize how much that would be helpful for her.

So, – I said – it's not that I think people shouldn't buy properties. I believe Real Estate is an excellent source of diversification, especially because it is a non-financial investment. Nothing prevents the investment, if made at the right time, from yielding as much as or even more than good financial investments, especially at times when the interest rates are low. It is not normal, but sometimes it happens.

But the point is less whether investing in Real Estate is good or not, but rather **when** it is good and when it is not.

Buying a property can bring to some degree, security and stability for your life. But acquiring a debt for 30+ years without even having a Safety Reserve can be anything but safe and stable.

The decision to buy a property can only be good if you have your financial life on track. That is why it is the last investment you want to think of.

And the way I see Real Estate is that it's actually a mix of an investment with an expense. Buying a house brings us some satisfaction, it is a big step and not everything we do in our lives can only be made thinking about money. It's good to know we are never going to be kicked off by a landlord, for example. It's good to know you can refurbish, break walls, build others, and spend money in keeping it modern and up to date, things that when you rent you usually don't do because you always think "I won't spend money to improve something that is not mine".

And then – I repeated to her – it just cannot be seen as a good investment since it is the only one you'll have for a good while and, thus, it is not even a pure investment.

Her face started to change, and I knew she was getting my point. I could have stopped right there, and I would get her convinced, but I had more to say.

And you know what? – I continued - you are not even married, you don't have kids and you don't know where you'll want to live then… probably, this house is not going to fit all your needs in the upcoming years.

Rather, save for the short- and medium-term expenses, build your Safety Reserve, make room in your budget to invest for your retirement and start building up wealth to generate additional income. Then, - and only then - should you consider investing in Real Estate.

It's the kind of thing that only pays off for some: those who know what they're doing. Anything other than that and the "dream" of home ownership can turn into a nightmare, and of the worst kind.

To conclude - I said, preparing for the grand finale – if you stop to think about it, everything you think you own, you actually kind of just rent. Life is short, Lilly. So, no matter if you think you are buying or renting your property, in reality you'll be just renting it anyway, renting for the time you are alive. We don't really own anything in life as it passes shortly, we rent it all. The difference is more related to paying all at once (buy) or in installments (rent). Depending on the phase in your life, you can choose whatever makes more sense to you.

There you go, and I had given my economic class to her and totally for free. I had covered all the issues in a simplified and direct way. – You're welcome, Lilly! - At that point, I knew that my explanation has changed her decision and more than that, it would probably even change the way she sees economic decisions in her life. I had accomplished my economist duty.

But, it turns out that instead, she looked at me, called me an insensible jerk to say all that when I knew she had decided to buy the apartment and we didn't speak to each other until the end of that evening.

Ah! And she bought the apartment anyway.

Can you believe that?

Jesus, people can get really sensitive when it comes to buying their own property!

Buying a house requires a lot more than rational decision making. There is just so many emotions involved. It is a symbol a success in our days. Think about it, when we refer to other people's financial success, we usually make use of the real estate success rule to measure it. It's hard to know how much of financial assets our friends have, but we all know how many properties they own. So, we use that to measure their level of financial success. Not rare, these people don't have anything other than that. No retirement funds, no safety reserve, no savings for short- and mid-term expenses, no stocks or bonds, no nothing else. And sometimes, they don't even care about becoming rich, they care about looking rich. They want to show the world their achievements. It is not rational.

And that conversation I and Lily had in the restaurant (more like a monologue)? Well, it actually never happened. I made it up. I don't even know any Lilly. But who cares? It could have happened, right? And, more importantly, I could use that invented story to make my point.

Accounting for Real Estate in Financial Planning Worksheet

Now, when it comes to booking the cash out of your mortgage or savings for the down payment, one question that comes to mind is: should I see it as an investment or as an expense?

I see 3 main possibilities, ranging from most simplified approaches to a more complex one, but that is also more accurate.

1) **Book it as an expense:** if you think that the main reason why you decided to buy a house was more related to meeting a consumption goal rather than an investing one, you can simplify it and book all cash out as an expense. In this case, the money you set aside for the down payment should be savings for short/mid-term expense and mortgage, a recurring expense. I recommend this approach to be used only if you actually live in the house you bought (or intend to live in the house you're saving money to buy).

2) **Book it as an investment:** that's the case when you bought the property more for investing reasons. This is better when you don't live in the house you bought, but instead you rent it to someone else. All cash out will be seen as investment and the cash-in from rent, as Income from Investment.

1) **Expense and Income + Investment:** This is my favorite approach for people that live in the house they are paying for. I understand it might bring a certain level of complexity, but it will be more transparent and accurate. As usually a house you're buying to live at is a mix of investment and expense, I suggest your spreadsheet reflects that. As I said before, we all pay to live, there will always be housing costs. What changes is that you can decide to pay this expense all at once, in case you decide to buy your house; or, as you go, if you decide to rent. So, I suggest you always book an amount of rent in your worksheet even if the house is yours. Book a theoretical value of that rent. This amount is what you could earn if you decided to rent it to someone else. Then, you would also book the exact same amount as an Income from Investment. These 2 amounts combined will zero, I know, but you'll be tracking how much your cost of living really is; and how much your real estate investment is yielding. In addition, you'll book the entire amount of mortgage as an investment. So, let's take my emotive imaginary friend Lilly as an example. In her place, I would account the $1,200 (this amount is theoretical based on the market value of a potential rent) as a Rent Expense as well as Income from investment. Then, I would book the $2,000 of mortgage as Investment. Note there is no cash-out for the $1,200 of rent, but I would account for that anyway. In reality, the best way to see it is that I bought an apartment and I'm renting it to myself. It's not that I'm not occurring housing costs anymore, but that the return of the investment I made offsets that cost. To have a clear view of the housing costs I'm incurring, as well as the return of my investment, I

better put it in. This way I'll bring visibility to my investment return as well as for my standard of living. There is a cost of living in the house you are, even when it is yours: it is the opportunity cost. You could always decide to rent it to somebody else and earn that amount. If you are short in money, for example, a good option could be to rent your property to somebody else and move to a place where rent is cheaper. When you decide to live in your own house, you're giving up that rent income. It is a cost that you better account for. It's good to have this visibility because the "rent you're paying to yourself" could be a hidden expense that you would like to cut if you knew it existed. As I said, you could move to another place with a cheaper rent (for example of $800/month) and continue to earn the income from your property by renting it to someone else (receive the $1,200/month). It is an option! But you have to be aware of that.

If you found option #3 to be complicated, you can stick to #1, but #3 is for sure the most accurate way of seeing the whole story.

CHAPTER TWENTY-FOUR

The myth of the One Hit that will save you

It was around December 2017 and one of my best friends posed this question in a WhatsApp group: "Who invests or has invested in Bitcoins?"

He is the type of guy who has never been interested in the Financial Markets, had never controlled his expenses nor has he ever budgeted anything. But now, he was simply fascinated with the return that some acquaintances have had "investing" in crypto currencies.

Right after, it was another friend's turn to send me a private message asking a question about it. Then another one... all in the same week. It was like that the entire week, people tagging me in Facebook news about the crypto currencies.

That week was preceding the launch of Bitcoin trades in the Chicago Board of Options Exchange and rumors were that other Exchanges could do the same.

For a week I tried to come up with tangible ways to explain how in my point of view, bets in Crypto Currencies seemed to me more like a pyramid scheme than a real investment.

Whoever follows the investment world knows the story of how Joe Kennedy, the father of US former President John F. Kennedy, avoided financial market losses in 1929. Legend has it that when he heard his shoeshine boy give him tips on what stocks to buy, he sold every stock he had. The unsolicited advice resulted in a life-changing moment for him. He promptly went back to his office and started unloading his stock portfolio. It was clear for him that no one there had any idea of what they were doing.

The history of bubbles is extremely old. It may seem ridiculous now looking at it in perspective, but in the seventeenth century the Dutch got into a frenzy by investing in tulips! Imagine changing your house for a plant? It sounds crazy, but it's real story.

In addition to the tulip bubble, there have been several different bubbles in the history of men and more recently a real estate bubble in the US that has caused the biggest economic crisis since 1929.

What is funny about this is that I even enjoy the idea of digital and private currencies that do not depend on central banks. I am totally in favor of currencies that are not subject to Monetary Policies.

But that is not the point here.

The point is that a currency should have three basic functions: 1) medium of exchange: be an intermediary between goods and services; 2) unit of account: be the instrument by which the goods are quoted; and 3) store of value: keep a stable purchase power over time.

Gentlemen, I can barely get a loaf on the corner with Bitcoins! What kind of currency is this? The speculator is all happy because there is a new bakery in NYC that has just started to accept payments in Bitcoin. Wow, what a hype! After more than 10 years of currency existence!

Even the Venezuelan Bolivar is more useful than that!

And honestly, people that transfer their money to their brokerage firms in order to buy crypto coins, do they do so because it is simpler to use these crypto coins instead of dollars or just because they speculate that there will be a gain from the appreciating value of the currency?

Everyone wants to resell it with profit, a typical financial pyramid in the bet that there will always be someone more fool than you to pay more.

Again, it doesn't mean that I do not believe in the power of crypto coins. I think they can be a very powerful tool. It's the current use that bothers me. As much as denouncing a Real Estate bubble would not make me against the existence of "houses"!

Come on, Bitcoin today is not a medium of exchange because the number of establishments that accept it may be increasing, but it is still very, very limited! It is not a unit of account because goods remain quoted in their values in traditional currencies. It is not a store of value because these crypto currencies' volatility creates huge swings in value.

Nothing against digital currencies, private currencies, etc. I repeat! They will be very welcome on the day when they become widely accepted. I will then use them very happily. But as a currency. On a daily basis for my day-to-day exchanges, just like any other currency. Not as an investment.

"... but Riko, these coins are the future."

It reminds me of the story I read in Alice Schroeder's book The Snowball about a presentation Warren Buffet made in 1999 at an annual investor meeting shortly before the dot-com bubble burst in the early 2000s in the US.

Some excerpts from Buffet's presentation that year:

"This is a 70-page list of the top US auto companies. There were more than 2,000 companies of this type in the USA: the automobile was probably the most important invention of the

first half of the twentieth century. It had a huge impact on people's lives. If, at the time of the first cars, you knew how the development of the country would be tied to them, they would have said, 'I need to get into that.'

But of those 2,000 original companies, according to last year's data, only 3 survived. And, all 3 were for sale for less than their book value, i.e. less than what was invested on them. So, cars had an impressive impact on Americans' lives. But it was not so positive for its investors.

Another great invention of the time was the first airplane. Between 1919 and 1939 there were about 200 aviation companies. Imagine if you had been visionary enough to imagine an unprecedented world. According to data from a few years ago, the set of all invested stocks in the history of aviation yielded zero dollars.

It looks wonderful to invest in new industries because they are very easy to promote. Conversely, defend investments in common products is very difficult. It's boring. It is much easier to promote exotic products, even if with losses because there is no quantitative parameter.

But people will continue to invest in them just like in the story of the oil prospector that arrives in Heaven. Hence St. Peter says: 'You cannot stay here. We keep all the miners behind that fence, and as you can see, it's full up, with no room for you.

'Then the oil prospector wisely shouts, 'They've discovered oil in hell.' Obviously, the lock of the fence breaks down and all miners rush to hell in the search for oil.

'Great trick,' says St. Peter, 'Now you have the whole room for you'. But the oil prospector then replies: 'I do not. I'm going to check out that Hell rumor. Maybe there is some truth in it after all'.

This is how people behave with investments. It's very easy to believe that a rumor has a bit of truth in it. "

The internet has completely changed our lives, but in 2000 several investors lost money on this investment in what now is known as the dot-com bubble. This was somehow also the embryo of what would become the 2008 Crisis.

In 1999, an investor in technology companies would say that Warren Buffet was old, outdated etc. In 2017, he is one of the 3 richest men in the world investing in established normal companies. Doing what any investor could do without having to be a "revolutionary visionary."

And yet, as I answered my friend, this story of revolutionary being the future is not always true. Prostitution is the oldest profession in the world and still yields a lot of money today.

But the magic of the new draws people who seek justification at any cost for their decisions.

"This time is different" is the well-known motto of economic bubbles in history, including the best seller of Carmen Reinhart and Kenneth Rogoff: "This time is different, eight centuries of financial deliriums" of 2009. In the book they show that in the end, all bubbles are similar and follow a cycle that can perfectly fit in the crypto currency history.

It is incredible what people are able to do in exchange for a promise to enrich in a magical way that does not involve work, effort, patience, methods and entrepreneurship.

Just watch how many people bet in the lottery every year certain that they will win! After all, for a cheap price, you can spend the rest of the week picturing yourself as a multimillionaire planning what you will do with the mountain of money which, in real life, you're probably never going to win. Soooo unproductive… time and energy that could be spent in actually producing stuff that could be beneficial to somebody else, and you.

"Yes, but you know, someone wins." Yes, you are right, someone wins lottery games. It just so happens that someone right now is also having a heart attack or being run over. And if you think that the chances of winning the Lottery are substantial, unfortunately the two latter probabilities are much higher. Except that you, reading this book right now, don't usually think about being run over.

That's the difference.

Most of the multi-millionaires in the world are self-made and they built it all by working in their own business. It was not a one-shot thing. Their wealth is a result of constant progress, steady method and rational decisions.

It is a process, not a one-hit wonder!

But it is a lot easier to believe in one shot.

Some years ago, the economists Levitt and Dubner wrote an article about "the myth of the successful drug dealer." In fact, they explain, only few of them actually get rich.

Most drug dealers earn very little, but remain in a highly risky jobs, encouraged by the hope that they will one day become rich and as powerful as their bosses.

This logic is not far from the reality of most employees, businessmen and investors.

For businesses, paying high salaries to executives is a great deal. These salaries are an incentive to increase productivity on the part of employees who will strive to try to someday reach these positions.

Great leaders in the commercial districts make use of this frequently. Some of them invest in nice cars, good suits, dinners at the best restaurants, but they do not do it for nothing. By passing on a successful image, they encourage their entire team to work hard and produce good results to increase their own standard of living.

People from Network Marketing companies do this very well. Everyone seems to be successful. Are they, really? Trust me, for some business leaders, spending can be an excellent investment.

Its' all about image!

In this context, lottery games are important to people. As life goes by, these games bring hope every Monday morning on the subway on the way to work when they swear that this week, they'll win.

CHAPTER TWENTY-FIVE

What it means to be rich?

Income is the most common measure of wealth used in the world. In the US is most commonly measured by United States Census Bureau in terms of both household or individual income and remains one of the most prominent indicators of class status.

Below, you'll find an example of this very simple and popular kind of calculation regarding total household income:

- Less than $30,000 per year, you are in the lowest income level.
- From $30,000 to $75,000, you are in the lower middle class.
- From $75,000 to $167,000, you are in the upper middle class
- More than $167,000 would place you in the upper class, knowing that with an annual income of more than $350,000 you are part of the 1% with highest income in the country.

According to this method, to know your social class, all you have to do is to consult the table.

For sure, you have checked to see what social class you are in, right?

Well, if yes, now forget that because this approach is very, very limited! The good thing, I admit, is that it is very simple, but the weakness is that it is totally bullshit!

Regarding the current income method, to elucidate how bad it is, I can say that an executive who earns $ 300,000, if dismissed, would be in a lower class than a junior analyst that makes $ 25,000. Even though the executive knows that in a few months he may be hired by a new firm.

It's not your income that defines how rich you are.

To measure one's wealth we must look at the person's Net Worth which indicates what that person is building in terms of wealth.

It's no use earning a lot and not having much because you've never built anything. High earnings can be offset by uncontrolled expenses.

Jeff Bezos, Warren Buffet and Bill Gates are not the richest guys in the world because they get the highest salaries. This is not how Forbes measures wealth.

Neither is it profit, believe it or not. These guys are among the richest men in the world because of their Net Worth. They own companies that are worth billions.

And you, what do you own? Forget how much you make, think of what you have built in terms of wealth in your entire life.

As I always say, you only manage what you measure, I then, invite you to follow the increase of your Net Worth. Something very simplified, but powerful. It is a simple account: assets - debt = Net Worth.

Now you'll have to lose the fear of the word "accounting". There is nothing complex in it. Assets are the things that you own such as real estate, a car or financial investments. Debt is the obligations you have like expenses that you have committed to pay in the future such as loans, for example.

A house is an asset. Its mortgage is a debt. The portion of your wealth coming from this house is the difference between how much it is worth and how much you still owe in terms of debt. If tomorrow you decide to sell it, how much will be left for you? This is your Net Worth.

In other words, your Net Worth is all that you have minus everything you owe.

It is a good idea to make your own balance sheet and follow it, to watch it grow. This is the true measure of wealth.

The balance amounts in savings accounts, bonds, funds and stocks are easy to check. An extract from your bank or broker are enough. For the value of your car, a good idea is to see how much an equivalent is being sold for in the market. Same thing for your house.

Regarding the debt, the ideal is that you bring them all to a present value, that is, how much they would cost if you decided to pay them all off today.

Simply adding up all the future installments may be a way for anyone who is unfamiliar with financial math but will give you a much worse result than the real one.

Of course, in the end, earning more tends to give you more opportunities to build a higher Net Worth, but how many opportunities are wasted every day?

How many people earn a high level of income and yet live indebted while so many others with financial intelligence build wealth from low salaries?

This whole book is about acquiring this financial intelligence that can leverage your financial situation. The growth of your Net Worth will be a consequence of good choices, good control and planning.

CHAPTER TWENTY-SIX

Financial Independence

Among all the elements money can bring us, one of the most desired is independence.

Look at all these guys dreaming about winning the lottery one day and moving to a Caribbean island. All they are actually dreaming of is to not have to work for money anymore. They want free time to be spent as they want.

We all want that!

The value of an asset depends directly on its scarcity and even though I know I have said that it is probably not tomorrow the day we encounter St. Peter in Heaven, the fact that we know that one day we will surely die turns time into one of the scarcest assets we have. Consequently, a valuable one.

Having free time is really important. As everything else, free time is not an innate right, but an achievement. And even if working is extremely important and honorable, it is best to work only because you want to and at what you want, like we have discussed in the chapter with the fisherman tale.

I'll repeat that as many times as I feel is needed, so take note: **Producing makes us feel useful, but it is one thing to work for pleasure, another, totally different, is to work for survival**.

At first, nobody has an option, we work because we have to, we have to create things, invent stuff, conquer independence and build wealth but living a lifetime this way is a choice.

Financial freedom is an opportunity that can be reached by those who have financial intelligence.

So, even better than monetary terms, the best measure of wealth is by the degree of financial independence.

Time is money. And vice versa.

So, you can turn any amount in USD or any other currency into a measure "in time" which is universal.

For this, all we need to know is how much our standard of life costs in monetary values by month. With this information in hand, we now know how much one month of our current living standard is worth.

Use the average of the last 12 months to offset seasonality effects. One year is a complete cycle where you will normally have spent not only your recurring expenses but all the expenses that you have only once a year.

This average cash out value will give you the dimension of how much it costs you to maintain your current living standard and once you know this magic number, you can measure other values in degree of financial independence.

For example, if you receive a net salary of $5,000 per month and your standard of living (your average monthly expenses in the last 12 months) is $ 2,500, this means that your salary is worth 2 months of financial independence. This measure is called the Coverage Ratio, which tells us nothing more than how long that amount could cover our standard of living in case we stopped receiving that income for a certain period of time.

The formula for calculating the Coverage Ratio in months is:

$$\frac{Amount\ in\ monetary\ terms}{Average\ Monthly\ Expenses\ in\ the\ last\ 12\ months}$$

To reach the amount in number of days, simply multiply the value found by 30.

How to use the Coverage Ratio

You can measure it in several ways. Here are some examples:

Total Coverage Ratio by Month:

$$\frac{Amount\ Invested\ in\ a\ given\ month}{Average\ Monthly\ Expenses\ in\ the\ last\ 12\ months}$$

This shows how much the amount you are investing in a given month is equivalent in terms of months.

But my favorite is the Net Worth Coverage Ratio, calculated through the following formula:

Net Worth Coverage Ratio by Month:

$$\frac{Total\ Net\ Worth}{Average\ Monthly\ Expenses\ of\ the\ last\ 12\ months}$$

In my view, this is the best measure of wealth available. It shows how much all the wealth you have built in your life translates into financial freedom for you.

A man with a net worth of $100,000 may automatically appear richer than one with a net worth of $50,000.

But if the former has average monthly expenditures of $20,000 while the latter, in contrast, spends only $5,000, the net-worth of the latter will mean 10 months of financial independence while that of the former, only 5.

Financial independence is expressed in levels, it is not binomial. You can have a high level of financial independence, a low or no independence at all. What many people refer to as financial independence is the one that shows an infinite coverage, that is when the passive income generated by your Net Worth would be able to pay all your monthly average expenses until you die.

But no one is financially independent without paying attention. The whole ratio suggests a stable standard of living. If it increases over time, independence will be shortened.

That is why you need to take good care of your expenses.

When I say that our standard of living may in some way imprison us is because it has a negative correlation with our Financial Freedom. The higher our costs of living is, the lower our independence is going to be. It is simple math.

I am not saying that you shouldn't seek a better quality of life. That's not it. By the way, there is no point in creating wealth and never being able to use it. But it's good that you know that it has a cost. It costs you time and level of independence.

Spending more has a double effect on your level of Financial Independence. First, because an increase in spending necessarily reduces the amount of your free income to invest (and thus build more assets), and secondly, because by spending more, you raise your standard of living that could be more difficult to keep in the future.

I repeat, the increase in the standard of living is very positive, but only when it is done in a sustainable way. A sudden surge without any structure can wipe out all your other plans and your finances as a whole and readjusting the damage done is going to be very painful.

CHAPTER TWENTY-SEVEN

Very nice, but I'm in debt. Now, what?

Oh la-la! This book seems to have come a little late for you if that is the case, but better late than later.

To begin with, having debt doesn't directly mean that you are in debt. What matters most is your Net Worth in this case. Is it positive or negative? If it's positive, it means that you are not really in debt.

If the debt you have is the $200 thousand mortgage of a house worth $300,000, then you are not really in debt because you could always sell your house, pay the Mortgage and even get some money back.

Additionally, not all debt is bad. An important thing to say is that you should also identify what kind of debt you have. There are three main types.

- **Bad Debt:** all debt with a high level of interest generated usually by overconsuming. This is the type of Debt you should never have and your goal number one should be to pay it off completely and never create it again!
- **Ok Debt:** generally, a loan linked to a good purpose such as Student Loans or Mortgages. If you get to pay them in advance, the better, but these are the kind of debt that you can actually live with because their interest rates are normally not so high, and you have a return of the investment that was only made possible because of that debt. If you used student loan to go to University, most likely, your salary now is higher because of that. If you

used Mortgage to buy your home, now you don't have to pay rent.

- **Good Debt:** we usually think about debt as a bad thing, but in reality, it could also be good. All debt with no interest or that charges you an interest rate that is lower than what you could receive if you placed that money in a safe investment can be considered as good debt. They are rare, but they exist. Think of it this way, I'll make it dramatic just to make my point: if you received one million dollars to be paid back the next year with no interest, you could use that money to invest for a year, receive $20,000 as interest for it, and still use the principal to pay back your debt. Free money! That is not good, but great debt!

Now, what I'll say might be shocking, but it's key: More important than the quality of the debt you hold is what is behind that. **Debt is not the main issue, but it is usually the symptom of a biggest problem which is lack of financial control.** So, even if you use "good debt" - that can be seen as free money - to maintain bad consuming habits, this will hurt your financial situation. You are using good debt for a horrible purpose transforming it in a terrifying debt.

Debt is generated by the use of wealth that you haven't created yet. This is very harmful for your life. And I really don't know how I could be clearer than that: **Do not spend more than you make!**

If you are in debt or maybe not yet, but your balance is often in negative meaning that sooner than later you will be in a complicated situation, here is what you have to do.

1. **Realize there is no magic solution for money problems**. Math is exact science: You will have to change your life and cut expenses. There is no other way out.
2. **You must decide on no more debt**. Once you've made a decision to change, you need to be able to begin the change immediately.

3. **Get rid of your credit cards now!** I won't lie, credit cards and home equity lines of credit can be very nice for people with their finances under control. If you are in debt, cut it all mercilessly! No more auto loans, no new TV or kitchen counter tops. No more store credit cards to buy clothing and no going on a trip for vacation this year.
4. **Create your Budget for the year and stick to it**. It must be realistic, but it must also have surplus for paying the existing debt.
5. **Forget about savings for a moment**, the best investment you can make now is pay off your debt.
6. **Pay your debt starting from the one with the highest interest rates** to the one with the lowest.
7. **Look for additional sources of income.** Your current income might not be enough to give you the lifestyle you want. In the short term, it doesn't matter though, you should make your expenses fit into what you currently make and not into a certain lifestyle you think you deserve just because your close friends and family have it. But, once you have your expenses under control, look for a better job or a raise. Temporarily you might even get an extra part-time job to increase your current income.

All that depends on the level and the type of debt you're in. If it's sustainable and you can pay for it as well as for your monthly expenses, there is no need to freak out.

If you can't and you're constantly closing your month in red, you better get strict right now, you probably passed the yellow sign.

If you feel it's completely out of control and snowballing, take your time to think and reason. Go through the 7 steps I mentioned above. If not enough, think about selling your financial assets if you have them. Even your house could be an idea, a little extreme, but a game changer. And remember, sometimes in life we have to take a step back in order to take two steps forward in the future. If you're going to get rid of your assets, you must be really committed about changing your life.

In this case, I hope you read once again this book, and more than that, keep reading other books about Personal Finance. It will help you keep your financial mindset sharp.

This change has to be a family commitment. It's important to point out how key it is that you sit down and talk with your significant other (if you have one, of course) and make the decision that your lives are going to change forever. A lot of people talk about how to change their financial lives, but never touch on the fact that if their husbands or spouses are not ready to change, it isn't going to happen.

CHAPTER TWENTY-EIGHT

Bonus: Financial Spreadsheet

To sum-up everything we have been talking about here, it's time to discuss your Financial Planning tool.

Microsoft Excel remains my favorite tool for financial control. People that prefer using apps than Excel say the greatest advantage of an app is that you have it with you wherever you are.

However, I don't think you really need to stay 24 hours a day connected to your Financial Planning and taking notes of everything you have spent in real time. This could be interesting in the beginning for the ones whose spending is completely out of control. Once you have organized your financial life, you don't need more than 5 minutes a day to update your sheet.

Excel has a great advantage: It is very flexible and user friendly. By typing in all my income and expenses, I feel I'm having a more accurate control of where my money is going to. I see expense by expense and classify them accordingly, instead of having a program doing that for me.

It's up to you to choose, if you feel good using an app, go for it! The most important thing is that you need some kind of control even if it's in a notebook. If so, buy a new one just for this purpose.

Here I'll share with you a free version of the Financial Spreadsheet I use. For you at this point everything is going to be very simple to understand. It consists basically in 3 sheets for each year of **Financial Planning**, where you'll have your Budget and Actual month by month divided into 1) Income; 2) Recurring Expenses; 3) Savings for Short/Mid Term Expenses and 4) Long Term Investments and a little Summary with a Recurring Coverage Ratio. Then, you'll have a dedicated sheet just to manage your **Savings for the Short and Mid Term Expenses** and a final one for your **Investments**.

It's simplified, but it's all you'll need in the beginning. Going forward, you should upgrade it to have full control of your financial position with your Net Worth and a more detailed control of your Investments.

Here is the link for the download of your Financial Spreadsheet:

https://lifeplannings.com/2019/08/09/get-your-spreadsheet/

Start now!

I would like to end this book with a case-study I found knowledgeable from the author Raiam dos Santos, but it is originally from the book "Art & Fear" written by David Bayles.

It's known as the 50-pound theory and it began as a case study of an American arts teacher who decided to do a social experiment inside his clay class.

He divided his students into two groups. In the first group, the goal was that in 3 months they would have to deliver the best clay vase they could. The grade would exclusively depend on the quality of this one vase. For this first group, the focus was on the masterpiece, the detail, the perfection.

With the rest of the class, he acted differently. The goal was to deliver 50 pounds of clay art in the same 3 months, no matter if the vases were nice or ugly. If 50 pounds of art were delivered, the group would get the top grade. Period.

After 3 months, the teacher distributed the grades and, to his surprise, all the masterpieces had come from the 50-pound group, those that focused on quantity rather than in quality.

Why?

Very simple: Practice leads to perfection and repetition generates mastery.

A normal clay vase they were used to making weighed less than 1 pound. To reach the 50 pounds, the second group had to really work hard every day.

The thought was not "I need to create the perfect vase", but "I need to act before my time runs out." And what happens when you work hard with consistency and repetition? You get better and better.

On the other hand, perfectionism breeds insecurity and anxiety.

Knowing that it would be judged on quality, the first group spent the whole quarter sitting around conceptualizing, thinking, devising how the perfect clay vase would have to be without ever having made any clay vase ever.

When it came time for practice, only trash came out!

While this group spent the entire quarter thinking about what they were going to do, the other group spent the entire quarter doing.

This example is a good illustration of everything discussed in this book. I talked about how you should organize your financial life, I said you need to save for every expense you plan to have in the near future, that you should invest to create a Safety Reserve, your Retirement Fund, and additional source of income. But, if you want to get something important out of this book, this one thing is **start today**.

I know it's rainy or maybe too sunny, or perhaps today is Thursday and you'll promise you'll take a look at all that in the weekend…

But start today. Small movements in the right direction are better than no movement at all. Some people will spend their lives waiting for the perfect time. There is no perfect time! There is the best time, and the best time is always now.

There is a great energy associated with living your path and dreams out loud. It's easy to be a critic and to use your own inability to move the needle forward on your vision to attack others playing the game. However, time will pass and one day you'll wake up wondering why you spent that finite resource called time just watching somebody else living out their dreams. You won't learn invaluable skills when seated in front of your TV watching other people play and pointing out your finger when they do it wrong. People who are actually in the arena is not there to please watchers. It is not only impossible to please everybody all the time, it is also absolutely unnecessary. Some people will be there to judge you no matter what you do. Do you want to know why? Because they have been infected with this illness called perfectionism and if they think they can't do it perfectly at first, then they can't do it at all.

And so, you come in, and you simply do it. Will there be flaws? Hell, yes! Will they stop you? No way! And they look at you and say: *who tha hell does that guy think he is*? *"How dare he?"*. For them, you were not supposed even try to do anything if you couldn't do it right at the first time. But as Malcolm Gladwell says, practice is not the thing you do once you're good. It's the thing you do that makes you good.

Look at me now. Fast forward a little more than 2 years from those days I was in Biarritz, from the time this book started to evolve in my mind. It's summertime 2019, and I'm at the charming neighborhood of Saint-Germain des Près in Paris. Ok, I'm still wearing a Quiksilver T-shirt what reminds me a little of the old days. But I'm here, exactly where I wanted to be, drinking a Saint Germain Spritz in the well-known *Les Deux Magots*, a *Café Litéraire* where many different famous and successful authors have been to do the same thing I am doing.

And it is no coincidence I ended up here. 2 years ago, Biarritz was my fisherman village - a great one, I confess - and I had the option to be a fisherman for the rest of my life. There is absolutely nothing wrong with that choice. It could have been an amazing choice for somebody. Not for me, at least not yet. I decided to be the fisherman who leaves the village to leverage my fishing business. And guess what: You are right now "having a fish" that most likely wouldn't have existed if I had decided to spend my weekends just surfing.

I am where I decided to be! It was anything but easy and sure. Sometimes, my wife Alice and I thought about giving up, we considered changing the plan... fortunately we didn't. We stuck to the plan. We did it because there was a plan in the first place. It's basic, but most people don't even have it, not a clear one. If only they knew how magical it is to accomplish your goals. How they look so huge from afar and all you're able to do is take some tiny little steps. And that's why a lot of people give up along the way. They see no progress or very little progress, not fast enough to keep them motivated.

That will certainly happen to you too, sorry to tell you, but the truth is that we don't change 180° from one day to the other. While organizing your financial life, you'll make some mistakes. Maybe you'll spend money on something you shouldn't because it wasn't in your budget, or you'll forget to take note and account for your expenses for a few days in row. When that happens don't get unmotivated. Change is a process. You'll need discipline and keep trying your best. Don't give up, don't freak out. Search for the baby steps along the way. Keep going and when you look back, you'll see how far you got. Scratch the word perfectionism from your life. It blocks you. Just face it, changes come from structural and sustainable ways.

I once had this conversation with a workmate who was telling me that she was paying gym so that she could work out at least three times a week, but because time was short, she never really got to go to the gym. So, I suggested she started going once a week on Saturday mornings. She replied "Once a week? What is the point?". People prefer to dream about the perfect scenario than actually start putting in practice what is possible. They think they are able to move to a perfect world in a blink of an eye.

The goal of this book is to change you, once it happens, your entire life will begin to change as a consequence.

When I decided to write this book, I committed to writing the best book that I could write. A perfect book? No way... there isn't such a book, and even if possible, come on, it would be awful. This is what makes us humans.

Now, after this long journey - I hope an enriching one - it's time to say goodbye. It was a pleasure spending this time with you in this very valuable and enjoyable conversation. Thanks for listening and sorry if I sometimes speak a lot, that's what my wife always tells me.

See you soon. It's now time to rise and grind.

Riko H. A. Jr.

"Utopia is on the horizon. I move two steps closer; it moves two steps further away. I walk another ten steps and the horizon runs ten steps further away. As much as I may walk, I'll never reach it. So, what's the point of Utopia?

The point is this: to keep walking."

(Eduardo Galeano)

APPENDIX I

Restart the Cycle

Now that we have discussed pretty much the entire financial cycle from income to expenses passing by debt, savings and investments, do you mind going back to income for a sec?

This book is a guidebook for your financial life with a detailed step by step formula for getting your finance on track. I feel it is so straight forward that it could only be closer to your reality if I called you by your first name.

So, don't read it just once. Instead, re-read it as your financial life evolves and I promise you that every time you read it, it will bring clarity to the phase you'll be living.

You know, our lives are made of financial cycles. Some people will live all their lives in a vicious circle – what Robert Kiyosaki calls the rat race. Others will choose the virtue one.

A new financial cycle begins with a new discussion about income. For that, it's important to know the difference between profit and Revenue. When you hear that Company X, Y or Z has made $50 million of revenues, not necessarily this Company has closed its Balance in positive. What matters in the end of the day, be it a Company, just one person or a family, is the difference between what you make and what you spend. This is your profit.

This is the idea of paying yourself first, building the virtue circle. Once you realize that, your life will change, you'll see an extra meaning on your work, on the money you manage and everything you own.

Earnings are not really the major problem for most people, but what they do out of the money they make. In most cases, this is the real issue. What I passed here throughout the last pages of this book is a financial housekeeping. You have to clean up the house first!

When I first talked about Income, I considered you had to stick to what you were currently having as income. So, my advice was that you had to stretch your living standard to fit into that. You should focus on organizing your financial life, acquire the correct mindset and find a way to keep a balanced life while investing to build an even better future.

If you don't do this housekeeping first, no matter how much you earn, you'll always be in trouble and that will end up demotivating you.

This is the worst that can happen, and, unfortunately is very – very – common. We often see that person earning 30 thousand a year, dreaming how her life would be if she earned 50 thousand. Time passes and now she is making the 50 thousand, but it doesn't look that nice anymore. Now, she dreams about 80 thousand. She'll make it, but life won't feel any better. No matter how much she walks, she will always have that feeling of being stuck, not knowing what went wrong.

In return, she'll feel exhausted for working too much, earning as much as she wanted and feeling her life is stuck. As a consequence, she'll start believing that this is life. *C'est la vie*, in its worst meaning. And then, she gives up.

This is why my focus was first on controlling your expenses and preparing your investments strategies. You have to be prepared to earn more.

Once you have your budget, you have spent some time to think about how you want to spend your money and how your life possibly has to change in the near future so that you can construct the basis of a greater one, now everything is the right place. It's time to move the needle forward and climb a step up.

Increase your income!

There is no need to think like crazy about making more money. Don't go out there chasing butterflies, just take care of your garden and the butterflies will naturally come. Once you set your planning, you'll see things changing in your life.

Controlling expenses is the unavoidable step, but until you reach a point where you can't go any further. If you make $30 thousand a year, it doesn't matter how less you spend, you'll always be limited to actively bringing in that amount of wealth. Controlling expenses is your defense.

Once you have stretched your expenses as much as you could, now you are ready to begin a new cycle: increasing your income. That is playing offense!

There are lots of different ways of bringing in additional income to your life.

- Sell stuff you don't need
- Drive an Uber
- Announce in Airbnb a room you don't use
- Deliver foods for Uber Eats
- Offer Baby sitter services in your neighborhood
- Walk Dogs
- Offer some kind of service in Fiverr

I have a friend who has transformed his house into a delivery pizza place. His pizzeria only works at night, when most people order it. He works in another job during the day, and when he gets home, the second shift starts. He answers phone calls, and he bakes these pizzas in his kitchen. All he had to invest was a nice industrial oven. No expenses with renting a place and no staff needed. It brings him additional money working from the comfort of his house from 7pm to 10pm. Why not?

All this is valid for people who want to earn more and for those who don't make much money. This will kill the excuse of the guy who says he cannot make ends meet just because of his low income. There are several opportunities out there. Don't want to do it? Well, one thing is to admit you don't want to because you have a better plan. Another one is saying you can't because bla bla bla.

Give reasons, not excuses.

Don't bring up excuses. Look at gaining money as a return back to the good service you have been offering to the entire society. Think of the reasons why one guy decided to open a bakery shop in your neighborhood. All that he can see is the reasons why he selfishly wanted to get money out of his baking skills. But by opening that shop, without realizing it, he actually benefited the entire neighborhood. They are all potential customers, glad to have commerce near home.

Again, if you are to take one thing from this book, it's that the only way you can ever be successful is by helping others accomplish their wants and needs.

Or as Peter Drucker once said to the book author Jim Collins, is never focus on being successful. Focus on being useful. Success is not a reason, it's a consequence.

Financial Level

Now you have enough information to start planning and controlling your current financial position. You'll be able to evolve and climb in your financial life. I suggest you start tracking where you stand now and head to the next step.

Step #1 Take a sit and write down in the Spreadsheet your Budget for the following months. Ideally plan 1 year ahead. Make room for paying your debt and Invest. Don't give up until you have decided to cut expenses until they all fit in your budget.

Step #2 Start controlling all your expenses in the Spreadsheet.

Step #3 Get rid of all of your Bad Debt. Start from the most expensive (higher interest rate) to the least expensive one.

Step #4 Start Saving for Short Term Mandatory Expenses

Step #5 Save 1/3 of your Safety Reserved need (let's say the equivalent of 2 months of average expenses for the ones that need to have 6 a reserve of months). Continue investing until you reach 100% of what's needed.

Step #6 Start saving for your retirement. If your employer offers a 401k match, take full advantage of it until you get full match.

Step #7 Create an investment account and buy ETFs of Stocks and Bonds.

Step #8 Achievement of the total Safety Reserve. Now you can start saving for a down payment of your own home (not mandatory).

What's next?

It doesn't stop here. Financial Education is a continuous process. As I promised in the book, there is a short list of book recommendations I would like to share with you. They vary from investment to self-development, but all classics! If you haven't read any of them, I strongly recommend you start right after updating your Financial Spreadsheet.

1.   Think and Grow Rich, Napoleon Hill.

2.   The richest man in Babylon, George S. Clason

3.   The Compound Effect, Darren Hardy

4.　　The 7 Habits of Highly Effective People: Powerful Lessons in Personal Change, Stephen R. Covey

5.　　Mindset: The New Psychology of Success, Carol Dweck

6.　　The Power of Habit: Why We Do What We Do in Life and Business, Charles Duhigg

7.　　The ONE Thing: The Surprisingly Simple Truth Behind Extraordinary Results, Gary Keller

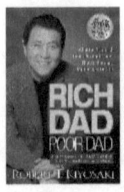

8.　　　<u>Rich Dad, Poor Dad, Robert Kiyosaki</u>

Acknowledgments

This book is a labor of love. It was a work that took many days and nights. I thank first of all my wife Alice for her patience (well, most of the times) and for my kids Anna and Vickie for being there and making me smile in the cloudy and rainy Parisian days when I saw myself locked in a room for several hours just writing, reading and rewriting all of this work.

I thank everyone who has read and bought my earlier works and encouraged me on this journey. The path was planned but the outcome was way better than I could have imagined. Thank you all for that.

A special thank you for my friend Buchner who not only advertised proudly my book, but also have gave me constant feedback on what to change and how to improve it. He is someone I learnt a lot from. Another great friend I'd also like to thank is Leo Souza, who used to be a surf mate but turned out to be a friend for life. He probably doesn't know it, but he was actually the guy who gave me the idea of building this book.

Lastly and mostly, I'd like to thank my parents for everything. They are simply the best people I've ever known and I am very lucky that this happy couple with amazing energy are my parents. They have always been supportive and positive.

And all of my friends in Brazil, the great ones I made in Bordeaux, my MBA classmates, the readers of my blog and so on. Every piece of good energy has played a part in this book and I'm willing to give it back – greater, if possible - to the world.

Some people say it is from Shakespeare, other from Picasso. It doesn't really matter. Now, I make them mine:

"The meaning of life is to find your gift. The purpose of life is to give it away."

About the Author

Riko H. A. Jr. is a personal finance and investments author. Originally from Barra da Tijuca, Rio de Janeiro, Brazil, he graduated in Economics and International Relations, and has an MBA in Finance with more than a decade of experience in Financial Departments of Large Multinational Companies.

His goal is to make people realize how important financial control is. Companies understand that very well and that's why they spend so much money to retain expensive financial departments. It pays off. But there is nothing a Company needs that a family doesn't. He tries to simplify all the Corporate Finance and adapt it to everyday life.

For Riko H. A. Jr. not everybody has to be rich to find joy, and even if a healthy financial life is important to everyone – even for the ones that don't strive to become rich – following the path of financial control is, ultimately, an individual choice.

Not everyone is obliged to do it.

But he dreams of the day when everyone will at least have the option of doing so.

www.ingramcontent.com/pod-product-compliance
Lightning Source LLC
Chambersburg PA
CBHW031836170526
45157CB00001B/322